# THE
# LIONS'
# LEGACY

# THE — LIONS' LEGACY

Working with
George Adamson
and the
lions of Africa

## GARETH PATTERSON

Robson Books

First published in Great Britain in 1991 by
Robson Books Ltd, Bolsover House,
5–6 Clipstone Street, London W1P 7EB

**British Library Cataloguing in Publication Data**

Patterson, Gareth
The lions' legacy : working with George Adamson
and the lions of Africa.
I. Title
639.9092

ISBN 0 86051 775 6

Photoset in North Wales by
Derek Doyle & Associates, Mold, Clwyd.
Printed in Great Britain by
WBC Print and WBC Bookbinders,
Bridgend, Glamorgan.

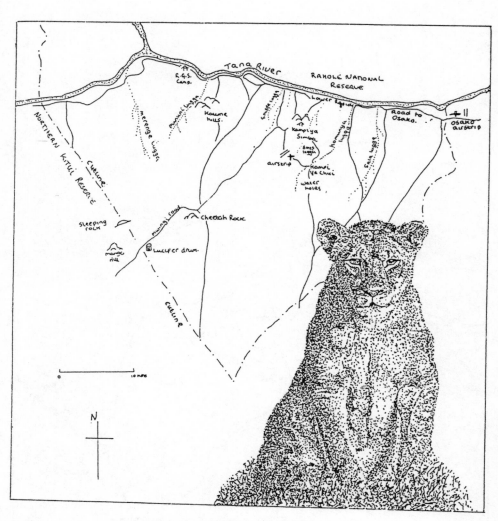

KORA NATIONAL RESERVE

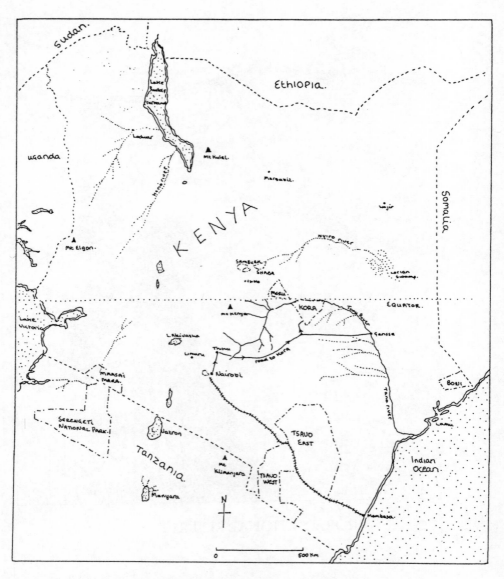

KENYA – Showing National Parks and Game Reserves

# Contents

# Foreword

## by Virginia McKenna

Hundreds and hundreds of people visited George Adamson's camp at Kora during the nineteen years he lived there. Hundreds and hundreds of words have been written about him. But it seems there is always something new to say, each person finding a new dimension to the experience — perhaps because to each person the visit was intensely personal.

Gareth's discovery of George's world, through reading his book, *Bwana Game*, as a young boy, led him inexorably to their meeting just over twelve years later in 1988. The old man's passion for lions and his deep understanding of their nature was reflected in the young man's own perception of the king of beasts. Both respected the lion's character and its place in nature's hierarchy. Both wished to share their lives with this great predator. Both have had their wish fulfilled.

Although Gareth knew George for only a few months, their deep and mutual concern for the wilderness of Kora and the creatures and plant life it contained, and their extraordinary rapport with lions, established a spiritual bond which continues today, two years after George's brutal murder.

On George's death the three young lions at Kora which he was rehabilitating back to the wild were suddenly left without their 'teacher'. Their father figure. For Gareth there was now only one path to tread – a path he would share with his new 'family' – though not, sadly, in the wilds of Kora, where George's other lions still haunt the river bank and move silently through the sea of thorn trees.

George's body may be buried at *Kampi ya Simba* but his spirit is everywhere, touching all of us who knew him – whether through his books or in person. And guiding and inspiring Gareth as he, in his turn, dedicates his life to lions – and to protecting animals and their future in the wild.

*Virginia McKenna*

# ◄ ◆ ► 

# Author's Note

During and after the writing of the first draft of this book I felt an uneasiness. Was it not presumptuous of me to write about George Adamson and the short time I knew him? Did I have a deep enough insight into George and his life? Time, reflection and rewriting has now dismissed that uneasiness and I wish to explain how.

I did not know George Adamson for long and, because of this, I cannot claim to have a 'biographer's' understanding of the man. Mine is a different understanding, an understanding which has developed since his death as I have continued the work with his three lions.

Many people knew and loved George for long years. Hundreds of people, visitors from diverse backgrounds, were enriched by meeting George at his home, Kora. There are also thousands of people who never met George but were nevertheless influenced or inspired by what they heard of him. Such was the powerful aura of a living legend.

I, though, did meet George and was privileged, for six short months, to have entered a portion of his unique world. The lion, the animal which represents his and my life's work, was the catalyst of our meeting, the lion kindled the flames of our friendship and the lion has resulted in the life that I live today.

Because of our fascination and great concern (some would say fanaticism) for the lion, the symbol of the free wilderness, I feel that my insight into George's life has some uniqueness. The uneasiness has been dispelled. I have written a story of George Adamson, of events which occurred in his long life, but particularly of those situations that surrounded him in the twilight time, a time of which I was a part.

Today, my life is merged with the lives of George's three lions, three young lions whom, after his death, I led from an uncertain future in Kenya to a free life in the Botswana bushlands. Because of the situation in which I live, my perception of the old man's determination has deepened. George died for life, typically protecting life which was threatened.

George's legacy is a testament to him. His legacy takes on a myriad of forms, influencing as he did people's attitudes, beliefs and actions. His legacy is embodied in animals free and wild, and reflected in the wild lands where still today the natural cycle of life exists as it always has and, one prays, always will.

Gareth Patterson

# Prologue

The lions had arrived, their presence announced only by the soft sound of low calls between the pride members, their forms shadowy in the typical inky African night. George Adamson turned his head to the sound and, as I touched the switch of the floodlight, the milling forms of eight lions could be seen outside the camp.

'Letea nyama,' George called (Bring meat), without turning from the lions. A gentle murmur of African voices could be heard from the darkened shadows of the staff quarters. 'Simba waliafike,' (The lions have come).

A tracker, tall and stately, his waist and shoulders swathed in local cotton cloth, his only adornment a traditional long-handled knife hanging from a leather belt, appeared with the meat box.

George rose and walked towards a small door in the protective lion-proof fence which skirted the camp. Slowly he pulled back the bolt and pushed the door open. He seized a chunk of dripping meat from the tracker and, with great deliberation, stepped down to a slab of stone and began calling to his lions, 'Growe. Come old Growe. Look.'

The silent form of a lioness moved from concealment beyond the circle of yellow light and padded on to the unique African stage.

She appeared to float forward, massive, sleek and powerful, possessed of the grace typical of the females of her kind. Here, in the isolated bush country of the Kora National Reserve, a man and beast, possessing kindred spirits, were once again meeting.

George continued to call to the lioness, and, when she was finally within three paces from where he stood, he flung the meat into the night air. The lioness sprang forward, seized the offering before it touched the ground and spun, head high, back into the darkness beyond the light's reach. Another lioness appeared from the shadows, and four ten-month-old cubs gambolled forward. Then, from behind a tree One Eye, another lioness, not possessing the calmness of spirit of the others, growled menacingly. Without any sign of concern, George turned and returned to the fence door, and threw meat to all the lions as they dashed forward in yellow flashes. All had come to feed – except one.

With a shake of his head George motioned to the tracker. '*Wapi Denis?*' he asked (Where is Denis?), and began scanning the bush with a powerful torch. Amber eyes reflected, like stars, from the camp rock. The three-year-old male, poised at the age of uncertainty, lay unmoving upon the stone.

One could sense George's affection for this young prince – affection perhaps inspired by memories of his lions of old, like Boy and Christian.

After being passed a chunk of flesh, George walked across the circle of light and, with concern and love, called almost impatiently to the lion, 'Look. Where's old Denis?' He walked until he had almost disappeared into the African night.

The thud of thrown meat hitting stony ground was heard, then the young lion erupted from his place upon the rock and, scarcely visible, bounded over to, and then over, the fallen meat until finally he stopped within two paces of George. He growled loudly at George before turning back to the meat, seizing it and shaking the sand clinging to it, and returned like a ghost to his place upon the rock. The young male had made his demonstration – a demonstration which was an attempt by the lion to be assertive towards George. Denis, the potential pride master, had reacted to George exactly as maturing lions do when, with caution, they attempt to rebuff an older but still respected male.

Later that night, as the staff slept soundly and the handful of visitors sat still in the calm of the evening, George placed his pipe upon the table and called to his lions once more, 'Come on, Growe. Come on,' and a dramatic rumble shook the quiet of the night as all eight lions replied, calling back with force to the *Baba ya Simba*, the Father of Lions. 'Umm … umm … umm … umm …. '

As the lions called, for a moment George chuckled to himself and then, seemingly embarrassed by the pride's reaction to his own voice, he returned to puff busily upon his pipe. He was privately delighted by the unique empathy and relationship he shared deeply with the lions. Though George did not murmur another word while the lions called, his contentment radiated strongly from him and was felt by all around this remarkable man.

# 1

◄ ♦ ►

# Lion Heart

This is the story of George Adamson, his lions and wilderness, and my privileged, enriching relationship with both – a short six-month adventure which was potentially to become my life's work.

My linking kinship with George Adamson began over fifteen years ago when I was a child growing up in the West African state of Nigeria.

On my twelfth birthday my mother gave me two things: the first, a copy of *Bwana Game*, George's autobiography; the second, a 'game reserve' – a wide board covered with painted papier-mâché hills, plains and waterholes. Great elephants of plastic roamed plains of paper and, on the edge of blue waterholes, painted zebras and antelope abounded. I was soon lost in a land of imaginary adventures; of brave

7

game wardens living with lions, and constantly in pursuit of destructive poachers.

I had grown up amongst the wildness of Africa from the sub-Saharan regions of northern Nigeria to the swampy lands of the south. I witnessed in East Africa, at a young age, part of the great migration of wildebeest, crashing across the Serengeti plains. I had seen snoozing lions in trees at Lake Manyara and run free as a growing boy amongst the slopes and streams of the Michiru mountains in Malawi.

I lived free and uninhibited, searching for animals with my African playmates. I was learning and living a natural education, an education of the people and animals of the land.

But, at the age of fourteen, convention stepped in. My marginal results at the local Malawian school banished me for two and a half years to a country I did not know, and still don't – Britain.

I was sent to southern England, to muddy fields, endless oppressive rain and new customs for a boy born British but loving only Africa. It was a tumultous period of awkwardness and heartache; full of dreams of fleeing, somehow, back to Africa. I achieved mediocre 'O' level results, and the image of a man in the wilderness, living amongst lions, remained in my mind.

From a cold, hollow, British classroom, I wrote a letter to George Adamson, and it was then that, for the first time, I wrote freely and uninhibitedly about my feelings for the wilds, Africa and my obsession to return to the continent.

George received the letter, and later passed it on to Joy Adamson who, unlike George, was looking for an assistant for her leopard study in the Shaba National Reserve.

At this time I had returned to Malawi on holiday and here, via Kenya and Britain, I received a letter from Joy.

She said that she was prepared, in principle, to take me on, to give me a chance to work with the leopard, Penny, Queen of Shaba. Joy instructed me to come to Kenya while she applied for my work permit. Those passionately written words from the classroom had somehow given me the chance I was yearning for.

I flew back to Britain elated, but such happiness was to be short-lived. Upon reaching London – by now ignoring the bustling people and stormy skies – I bought a newspaper and stood shocked and horrified as I read the headline, 'Joy Adamson Murdered'.

I had lost a dream, and the world had lost a voice from the wilderness. It was a voice whose words and deeds had captured the hearts of millions and created an awareness of the wilderness which has never since been surpassed.

Over the next few weeks, I mourned what had happened and, in the remote Kenyan bush, an old man with a mane of yellow-white hair stood over the grave of Elsa, his bond with Joy, and buried his wife's ashes under the stony slab.

Six months later I returned to Africa, perhaps now even more determined to make my quest a life's work and, at the age of eighteen, I began a career which would lead me to a love for lions, and ultimately to George Adamson.

I began as an apprentice game ranger in a private game reserve bordering the Kruger National Park in South Africa, and remember clearly my first encounter and education with lions.

Early one morning I was in the reserve with an experienced ranger, when an old lioness suddenly appeared and, without warning, tore towards our open vehicle. We were surrounded by thick bush and, while my companion was attempting to urge life into the ailing engine, the lioness bounded forward.

We had no firearm – only a stout length of wood.

Primeval instinct took over and with natural self-preservation I hollered and screamed at the lioness, banging the vehicle sides with the stick. The Land Rover eventually lurched forward and the lioness slowed down and stopped.

The lesson learned was to remain with me – respect the wild, but do not fear it, because fear fuels disaster.

From this apprentice stage I moved to work with Dr Ian Player of the Wilderness Leadership School. In a tumbledown farmhouse, perched in the foothills of the Drakensberg range, I lived with my co-worker and friend, Rozanne Savory. Here I was responsible for a sizeable spread of wild land. I would walk for miles checking fences, pulling up poachers' snares and shooting at their hunting dogs as Rozanne drummed up business for nature trails through an antiquated crank-up telephone. I was rapidly learning about the wilderness concept and part of my job was to pass on my love and concern for the wilds to the troops of children who visited the nature trails centre.

After a year I made a fortuitous move which found me in the big game bush country of the North East Tuli Block in Botswana. Here, through being instructed to instigate a study of an unknown lion population, my love and empathy for this great cat was born. For four years I spoke, wrote and dreamt about the animal which symbolized the African wilderness. I entered the lions' lives as deeply as they entered mine. I grew to know prides, and the lions themselves as individuals – shared their triumphs and suffered with them their persecution.

Through poaching and illegal hunting, I was to lose twenty-five lions in two and a half years from the reserve's regional population of fifty-five. I found my lions snared by poachers' traps – whenever possible, releasing them from the cruel wire – while others were shot by neighbouring South African farmers, who would lure my lions on to their farms and to their deaths, merely for sport.

The emotion and grief I felt while attempting to protect these cats resulted in my first book, *Cry for the Lions* – a call for the much-needed conservation of the lions of all Africa.

Today I feel that such emotion which I had expressed was uncannily similar to that which George felt at a similar stage of his life. Generations apart, we were both repulsed by the destruction of such animals. This is reflected in two passages from two books – his *Bwana Game* and my *Cry for the Lions*. George wrote:

One evening we came on a magnificent lioness on a rock, gazing out across the plains. She was sculptured by the setting sun, as though she were part of the granite on which she lay. I wondered how many lions had lain on the self-same rock during countless centuries while the human race was still in its cradle. It was a thought which made me reflect that though civilized man has spent untold treasure on preserving ancient buildings and works of art fashioned by the hand of man, yet he destroys these creatures which typify the perfection of ageless beauty and grace. And he does so for no better reason than to boast of a prowess achieved by means of a weapon designed by man to destroy man, or to use its skin to grace some graceless abode. In my mind's eye I could see the vast herds of wild creatures on these great plains swept away by progress, as they have been swept away in other lands and, in their stead, herds of degenerate livestock; it was a depressing vision.

Some twenty years after this piece was published, I wrote the following about one of my lions, slain and later mounted in a taxidermist's shop:

Its face had been moulded into a fearsome snarl, its body stiff and mis-shapen. The price tag stated three thousand rands. While the shell of a lion can be given a price, a living lion is surely priceless. It seems strange that a masterpiece created by man, an ancient sculpture, for example, is revered by him as a holy relic. However, a masterpiece created by nature, a lion, a form of life much older than the human race is still today destroyed for pleasure. Such is the strange way of some men.

My first meeting with George stemmed from a conversation with a friend of mine early in 1988. I was at this time researching material for my second book, *Where the*

*Lion Walked*, a work through which I wished to illustrate the largely unrecognized fact that the lion and Africa are reaching a disastrous dilemma. I had driven some twenty-two thousand kilometres through wild areas of southern Africa and had paused in Johannesburg to plan the final part of the project. My friend suggested that I should contact and visit George, as he knew of my deeply passionate feelings for the future of the lion in today's Africa and that by meeting George I would be able to speak freely and uninhibitedly about the lion as I knew the animal.

Prompted by this suggestion, I decided that the final chapter of the book would be a reflection on a different Africa to the one which, for six months, I had travelled through. I would write of the Africa of old which is quickly passing us by – George Adamson's Africa.

I wrote to George telling him of my work with lions and inquired as to whether I could visit him. In time I received a reply stating that I would certainly be welcomed at his camp and that he looked forward to hearing more about my work. Weeks later I passed on a message to George through friends in Nairobi that I would be visiting in June 1988.

Accompanied by my friend, Jane Hunter, who was assisting me with my project, we flew to Kenya. After a brief, but magical sojourn in the Masai Mara, we hired a Suzuki jeep in Nairobi and one morning, clutching hand-written directions on how to reach Kora, we set off.

Five hours after leaving Nairobi, we reached the southern boundary of the Kora Reserve. My first impression was one of shock at the desperately dry, over-grazed appearance of the reserve. Grass was virtually non-existent, represented only by sharp, dry tufts held by the baked ground. I knew that the area was overrun by nomadic Somali tribesmen and their herds of camels, cattle and goats, but the destruction caused by the desperate feeding of the livestock was frighteningly visible.

I thought to myself while driving through this isolated and

vulnerable reserve how sad it was that a man who had
dedicated his life to wildlife was now, in his twilight years,
living in an area which epitomized man's destruction of the
wilderness.

We reached *Kampi ya Simba*, George's home, in the early
evening. The camp, encircled by a lion-proof fence, seemed
empty and quiet as we drove up to the gate. Silently, one of
George's staff appeared to open the gate and I drove into the
camp with a feeling of excitement, merged with a slight tingle
of apprehension. After parking the vehicle, we were led by
the member of staff towards the largest of the collection of
palm-fronded buildings. As I walked, I saw through a gap in
the palm leaves covering the buildings, a glimpse of a mane of
white hair and the unmistakable profile of George Adamson.

As we reached the hut, George suddenly appeared. He was
dressed in his green shorts and had leather sandals on his feet.
At first, he looked at Jane and me with a puzzled expression
and in a somewhat formal fashion, I hastily introduced ourselves. Then George smiled, his face transformed, and the
characteristic sparkle in his eyes instantly put us at ease. 'Oh
yes,' he said, 'I remember your letter now. Would you like
some tea?' Another figure then appeared from the mess hut
and George introduced us to Margot Henke, an old friend of
Joy's and George's who was visiting the camp.

Soon we were settled down and quickly the conversation
turned to 'lion'. I remembered on that first meeting, the great
interest George took in the copy of my book, *Cry for the Lions*,
which I had brought for him. I told him more about my work
with the lions in Botswana and described the poaching problems. To this he reacted with a creased brow, his head shaking
despondently. As he murmured, 'Good God,' it was as
though he was grieving for my lions' deaths as he would grieve
for his own. This reaction was purely due to the fact that they
were lions – the animal he cares so deeply for.

The conversation in the mess hut was monopolized by
George and me as Jane and Margot quietly listened to our

discussions. The talk continued as the sun lowered to the horizon and as the African night sounds began – the 'pink-pink' of bats and the monotonous crickets' song. It was an evening of constant exchange of questions. George, in his answers, would verify my thoughts on lion behaviour and would inquire more about my lions in Botswana. As the night went on, he unfolded parts of his life-long experience with lions.

That first meeting with George proved my friend's suggestion correct – it was a remarkable experience for me. For the first time I was talking freely and completely about the lion without fear of the maligning scepticism of the blinkered or disbelieving scientist.

After a simple dinner of soup and toast and after Jane and Margot had retired to sleep, George and I began to talk at length about subjects such as telepathy between lions and the possible existence of such communication between man and lion. George listened as I described uncanny meetings between Darky, an old pride male of the North East Tuli Block and myself – meetings where a form of understanding and communication seemingly existed.

I recounted to George how, a year and a half before, when I was planning to leave the North East Tuli Block to write *Cry for the Lions* to publicize the plight of my lions, a strange encounter took place between Darky and me. I told how one morning in the reserve I had found this lion's tracks and followed them on foot as I had done almost every week for nearly four years. On this occasion though I felt, for the first time, a sense of foreboding. I followed the tracks across a dry riverbed, through the dark depths of riverine bush until finally, an hour later, the tracks led me on to a wide flood plain. I continued to follow Darky's tracks but the 'bad feeling' persisted. When I was half-way across the flood plain, I decided to return to the vehicle and continue the search from my Land Rover. As I turned and walked away, I suddenly heard in the distance sounds of crashing in the bush. I spun around to see Darky rushing out of the scrub towards me. He was dashing forward in long bounds, his mouth agape. I told George that evening that my first response to this was not fear, but anger – 'Why was he doing this to me?' The lion I had known so well and never feared was charging forward with an intent to maim or kill. The distance between us closed in a flash and I raised my rifle. When Darky was just twenty yards away, I fired over his head, praying that the report of the shot would turn him. The lion then sprang into the air, tore over a small acacia bush and disappeared into the thick bush with a volley of hoarse grunts.

I continued to tell George how shocked I was by this unusual aggression from Darky and how, at the time, I could not explain the attack. Lions generally fear man and if a lion is unseen by man on foot, it will not show itself, preferring to remain hidden. Darky had reacted in the opposite way. I had not seen him, was a long distance away, and was walking in the opposite direction from where he lay. I knew at the time that there must be an explanation for his behaviour.

After describing this incident to George, I suddenly felt a tingle of excitement as the realization of a possible explanation became clear. By his behaviour, Darky was charging towards me as he would to a competing predator, a leopard for example, or as he would to a rival male lion which had encroached into his territory. Because of my empathy for lions, was Darky reacting towards me as though I were a lion? Do lions see not only with their eyes but with their souls, perhaps recognizing me not as a man physically, but, in some form of interpretation, as having a lion's spirit? These were the questions kindled by my first meeting with George.

George, in response to my story, told me of some similar experiences he had had with lions. He told me, for example, how it was not unusual for his lions, second and third generation wild-born lions, offspring of those he had reared, after months away in the bush, to appear suddenly at the camp and present their cubs to him. This behaviour is normally reserved for the pride where, when cubs are about two months old, a lioness will introduce them to the pride members.

That first evening with George wonderfully strengthened my belief in the suspicions I had about man and lion, but which I had not spoken of before. While I spoke, George would nod indulgently and understandingly. Perhaps George too, for so long had been caged by the limited frontiers of what outsiders could accept and believe and thus, like me, could not express his true thoughts and feelings.

In the three days we spent at *Kampi ya Simba* George and I discussed other situations and experiences at length, moments that derive from an unflagging belief and insight into the lion and its world and on reflection, I believe that possibly this was one of the few times George recognized that someone else shared his empathy with the lion. The beginning of our closeness was thus kindled.

On our last night with George, he talked of how he would like to re-establish his lion rehabilitation work, a project which had been closed down by the authorities for eight long years. At the time of our visit he had just been granted permission by the Department of Wildlife to continue the work. Late that final evening he suggested that perhaps I would like to return to Kora after completing the work on my book to help him with his project.

'I am getting a touch old now, Gareth,' he added with the sparkle in his eyes. I sensed that he wanted to know more about me, and I in turn dearly wanted to learn and gain a greater insight into his thoughts and beliefs.

We then discussed how probable it would be for me to be granted a work permit but deliberately did not dwell too long on this, as I felt that George wanted to see my experience with lions for himself, before any hard decision was made. At George's offer, I decided then that I would return to Kora and see what would develop in the long term.

# 2

◄ ♦ ►

# The Grim Reapers

In August 1988 I had returned to Kenya and witnessed a wildlife crisis. I was returning to George and Kora as Somali bandits were sweeping across the country harassing the elephant herds to a degree unprecedented in years past, and conservationists and government officials were seriously concerned about the slaughter. On arriving in Nairobi I stayed with my friends, Joe and Simone Cheffings, who run the successful Bataleur Safaris. As I sat with Joe, a former professional hunter who had witnessed the winds of change, independence and the 1970s ban upon his profession, I saw that he was clearly discontented, the cause of this feeling being the elephant 'killing fields' in the Tsavo National Park. Joe, like many other safari operators, was shocked at the destruction caused by the armed gangs. Events were taking place that were not only destroying a wildlife heritage, but also mounting pressure upon the Government itself. In the past six months, over six hundred elephants had been shot in the Tsavo National Park, which left an estimated three hundred young calves defenceless, confused and ultimately vulnerable to predators like lion and hyena. The term 'roadsiders' had been coined by the shocked conservationists and safari operators – 'roadsiders' being elephant carcasses stripped of ivory and left decaying along Tsavo's dirt tracks. Their deaths suggested that Park officials were seriously implicated in the slaughter, for who else had easy access into the Park?

The Tsavo herds had been depleted from an estimated 17,487 to 4,337, a 75 per cent reduction in seventeen years. The *shifta* (the Kenyan term for the Somali bandits), whether staking out waterholes or firing blindly into herds, were contributing to a horrific animal tragedy reminiscent of the near extinction of the North American bison or the slaughter of the whales in the world's oceans. In addition, the political implications were strong, for the Somalis have never renounced their claim to the historical lands of eastern Kenya. They believe that the colonial criss-cross of boundary lines robbed them of their rightful land and split many of their countrymen. Some people would quietly agree with this but the Boran tribe believe otherwise and have a resentful story about how the Somali cleverly grasped parts of Kenya.

Long ago, the story goes, a Somali dying of thirst crossed the boundary and appeared at a Kenyan waterhole begging for permission to drink. Permission granted, he regained his strength and asked if he could call his wife to tend to his needs. Later, he asked if he could bring his livestock, his camels and cattle, to support him and again permission was given. Lastly, he asked if he might bring the family and relatives for whom he was responsible. Eventually, so great were the Somalis' numbers that the Boran were ordered out of the region and this, so the Boran say, with bitterness, is the foundation of the Somali claim to north-eastern Kenya.

Today, the Somalis, and their banditry, are not just apparent in Kenya. In a few short years they have infiltrated Tanzania and have even reached northern Mozambique, an incredible one thousand miles from their homeland, slaughtering elephants whenever possible.

What was happening to the elephants in Kenya had already happened to the black rhino. Kenya's remaining six hundred black rhino, out of the continent's population of 3,500, largely exist within large fenced areas on private land, protected, though not completely, by anti-poaching guards. I realized, as Joe spoke, that if the well-known parks such as Tsavo were under siege, then one could only wonder what was happening within Kora, George Adamson's territory. If the bandits were operating openly within areas of high tourism, then the damage must be devastating in the vulnerable and infrequently visited Kora Reserve. The Kora elephant herds must be virtually wiped out as the game department's enforcement, I had heard, was under-equipped and understaffed and there was no army presence in the reserve.

As I climbed into the light aircraft at Wilson Airport to leave for Kora, I remembered Joe's words, 'Take care Gareth. God only knows what's happening up at Kora.' I was soon to find out.

On the hour-long flight, criss-crossing the five dams upon the Tana River, I pondered about my return to Kora and what it might bring. Returning to George, to be with him, I felt was fulfilling an old African quest – respect for your elders and learning from their life and experiences. But it was to become much more than that.

Here, we must digress a little. For sixteen years, George had been joined in his work at Kora by Tony Fitzjohn. Tony had joined George at Kora at the age of twenty-six, and had been a godsend to him and his work. Over the years, Tony became known as an ultimate wild bush man who, it seemed, was either liked or disliked with equal passion. He was fearless when working with the lions and an expert when it came to keeping the old vehicles and machinery running. He also established his own rehabilitation project dealing with leopards and developed a rapport with these solitary cats which perhaps was as strong as George's empathy with lions. His work with George had been invaluable, but now, seemingly a victim of circumstances, he was unable to return to Kora because of a damaging rift between himself and some authorities. I do not know the details, nor did I ask them, but on board the plane with me was Kim Ellis, Tony Fitzjohn's partner, a striking, dark-haired American woman who was returning to Kora to discuss arrangements with George for their move to Tanzania. She and Tony were concentrating on wild dogs in that neighbouring territory. As Kim had bade Tony goodbye upon the tarmac at Wilson Airport on our way to Kora, the scene of the two of them together produced a feeling of sadness and regret which was almost tangible.

The plane droned on, with Kim Ellis pointing out landmarks to me, while young Dave Seaton expertly piloted us on our course to Kora. Dave pointed out two granite *inselbergs* (stone outcrops) in the distance and announced, 'Kora Rock straight ahead – we should be there in ten minutes or so.' Soon we were flipping flamboyantly between the stony valley of the twin rock outcrops and buzzed the camp. Dave, I realized later, used a plane like an extension of his own body and with a skill which defied his years. He banked the plane low over the small camp which looked singularly vulnerable in this great tawny expanse of thorn and rock.

I could see that the land was terribly dry and, when commenting on it, Kim told me that the area had had little over one and a half inches of rain the previous season. The scene below us was sadly familiar to me. Sadly, because the terrain was uncannily similar to the land I had entered several years previously, the North East Tuli Block, where my involvement with and concern for the lion had begun. Like Kora, the North East Tuli Block was badly over-grazed and some individuals felt that the damage was irreparable and largely induced by man's influences (fences restricting game movement, etc.) combined with natural drought cycles. It must be remembered that drought in Africa is an age-old, natural phenomenon which acts as a balancing factor and, in many respects, promotes life by stabilizing animal populations to the level at which the habitat can sustain them. But natural drought cycles, combined with man's interference such as overstocking of livestock and, in turn, over-grazing and the subsequent soil erosion, breaks links in the natural chain reaction and the region subsequently deteriorates as desertification is promoted, the waterholes lower and a change in vegetation takes place. All this occurs too quickly for adaptation to take place in the wildlife populations and a decline steadily sets in and affects all forms of life. I wondered as we flew low over the area whether this was also part of the Kora story.

The plane gently settled upon the strip which had been carved years before by George's brother, Terence, from the dense acacia/commiphora bush land, and soon we were bouncing along in an ancient Land Rover which was, in the months ahead, to become a home for me at Kora. George and his staff stood in the camp to greet us, while a scattering of white visitors, young and watchful, peered out at us from the various huts.

*Kampi ya Simba*, George's home for nineteen years, has been termed a 'zoo in reverse' which is an apt description of a camp designed to keep people in, and the big cats out. A tall wire fence encircles an assortment of so-called 'huts' — the buildings made entirely of local materials, with roofs of palm fronds, walls of hessian sacking and floors of river sand. On one side, behind George's workshop, is an orderly row of

huts which is his staff accommodation, and at the front of
the camp, next to the mess hut, adorned with pictures old
and new of George and his lions, is the territory of Hamissi,
the cook. His 'kitchen' consists of a small palm frond-
covered hut, outside which is a constantly burning fire
surrounded by an array of ancient, blackened kettles, pots
and fire grids. The camp is basic, but it contains all that
George requires, simple and functional.

At our last meeting I had told George that I would return
within two months and had done so, with work on the book
completed, almost to the day. George, dressed typically in
his green shorts and leather sandals, was pleased to see me, if
not a little surprised that I had returned as promptly as we
had planned.

When I had last left Kora, I left it as perhaps it should be,
with just a couple of visitors in camp and George at ease, but
this time, when I entered the mess hut, I felt strangely
claustrophobic at the assortment of visitors inhabiting his
home.

At camp, amongst others, was a used car salesman from
Worthing in England and a Negro woman trekking through
Africa searching for her African 'roots', and I sensed that
amongst some of the visitors, a form of hostility, jealousy
perhaps for George's attention, flowed between them. I also
sensed from George that the news of the activities of the
Somalis in Kenya and the destruction of the elephant herds
was also putting strain on him. After a lifetime of protecting
wildlife and the wilderness, perhaps he felt that his efforts
were in vain, as the changes in Africa continued to
determine the future and possible demise of the last
wilderness.

It was only on the second day at Kora that I witnessed, for
the first time, the product of human greed-inspired violence
which had erupted in this land. George told me on the first
night of the poaching taking place within Kora. Two
elephants had been shot recently by infiltrating Somali

bandits, militant men who had deserted from the civil war in their own land to venture into an equally grisly but economically more viable livelihood – ivory poaching.

The following day, four camp visitors and I, accompanied by two of the trackers, Abdi, George's 'lion boy' and Mohammed, went to seek the poachers' work. Beyond the airstrip we had landed upon the day before, unseen and veiled by the tangle of thick bush, lay the results of the bandits' work. We climbed out of the vehicle, and walked single file into the thorn country. I knew what to expect and my senses were sharpened. A dead elephant – and I had witnessed this in Botswana – is the ultimate in degradation of life. Everything the elephant possesses – its intelligence, its close family bond and unparalleled dignity – disappears at the report of shots and its grey form slumps heavily to the ground.

Mohammed, bush-wise, seized a rock as we neared the site of the tragedy, knowing only too well that the bodies would attract the principal meat-eaters, hyenas and lions. Through a clearing the grim scene suddenly came into view. Two pitiful mounds of grey lay, further defiled by streaks of vulture excrement. There was a cow and her calf, a female of perhaps only seven years. The carcasses were swollen hideously by the sun and by their own fermenting body juices. The cow was slumped, front legs splayed, body tipped forward with her chest heavily sunk into the stony ground. In her death throes her back legs had pushed backwards as life left her, leaving her as though in macabre prayer. The blood and body fluids spread slowly as congealing gradually took place. The bodies of mother and young lay less than nine feet apart and it was as if, in death, they were desperately reaching out to each other. In time, the two circles of corruption would meet and mingle. To me, this meeting would bond them symbolically in their tragic and untimely deaths, the mother and calf merged close in death as they were once merged in life.

Alone, I walked towards this familiar African scene. I was untroubled by the pungent smell and the work of the festooning maggots, but the elephants' deaths devastated me and evoked an emotion which I have too often experienced. From the signs upon the stony ground and from the scene itself, it was obvious that the bandits had moved in close, unseen by the mother and calf, who had been resting beneath the low trees in the searing heat of midday. Silently, the poachers would have approached, carefully aiming their weapons, G3s or AK 47s, and at a devastatingly close range, unleashed the weapons of death and I remembered, once again, George's words, ' ... achieved by means of a weapon designed by man to destroy man .... '

Mercifully it was clear that the killing was quick; both elephants lay where they had once stood, falling after hearing the blasts, and as the searing lead slammed repeatedly into their great bodies. Death had numbed their beings as their spirits were released, untimely, from their bodies.

This incident had occurred perhaps some five days before, and only the destruction of man and heat had changed the scene of the fallen elephants. I walked around the prostrate forms. Their trunks and heads had been slashed by axes – slicing the flesh from above the eyes. The ivory had been removed – ivory which was one day to become a carving, a figurine or perhaps rows of hundreds of trinkets or bracelets. The elephants' tusks, the youngster's tiny ivory, would be fashioned into pleasing objects in the eyes of the people in faraway lands, people who would not associate their purchased object of human vanity with the horror, death, the mounds of decaying flesh in the African bush.

As I photographed the scene I began to wonder how long it would be before we reached the end of the game – or have we already, without knowing it, reached this final point? The four visitors to George's camp had looked at the scene from a distance, the strong smell of death preventing them from coming closer. Mohammed and Abdi were searching for tracks on the perimeters of the scene, and I was glad to be alone. In mourning at this all too common African scene, I needed to be left alone in a cocoon of grief without forced situation-induced discussion – if only for a short while.

We left this tragic scene as the orange sun was filtering through the thorn country. Those with me, George's visitors, had unsuspectingly and unwillingly witnessed the horror erupting in the last years of Adamson's Africa. As I walked, my grief remained with me, for it was as if my blood, my African bonding with the land had stained the ground, and it is such blood-letting that drains Africa of its wilderness spirit.

I sensed the mood of the others. The image of the dead elephants had been forced into their minds, and this image, I hoped, would remain indelibly, for it was, and is, the unblemished truth, the reality of everyday occurrences in today's Africa which everyone could help prevent if they allowed conscience to determine their actions.

Later that evening when we approached camp, I saw that more visitors had arrived by aircraft from Nairobi. They were a young Australian couple trekking through Africa, and the Austrian doctor, Andrew Meyerhold, a dedicated supporter of Kora and George. Andrew is a kindly man, who has helped in many ways over the years at *Kampi ya Simba*.

The mood in the camp, however, was uneasy, partly because of the scene we had just left, but something else, unrecognizable, almost as if carried in the breeze, permeated the camp. The next day, an incident would take place which would affect each of us emotionally, and though we had no idea that evening of what was to occur, it was, in retrospect, as though the incident had already affected us and subdued all at *Kampi ya Simba*.

Unexpectedly, later that evening, George's lion pride arrived – the twelve-year-old lioness, Growe, another lioness, One Eye, and their offspring – a three-year-old male

and female and four ten-month-old cubs. I learnt in the
weeks ahead much about these lions who periodically visited
George – lions who lived natural lives in the Kora bush but
who, for many different reasons, returned to George at
*Kampi ya Simba*. They were wild-born lions and were all
related to the lions George had reared over the years.

Growe was the daughter of the lioness Gigi, who had been
brought to Kora from the Nairobi orphanage in 1974.
George reared her and, in August 1977, she mated with a
wild male lion who was named Blackantan. Three and a half
months later, she gave birth to the two sisters, Growe and
Glowe. Tragically, Glowe, like so many of George's lions,
was poisoned by the Somalis in 1984.

The uneasy feeling in camp became tinged with danger as
George let himself through the protective fence door to walk
outside the camp and feed the lions. I was to see George
with his lions on many occasions in the future, and was to
share with him the intimacy of being amongst the great cats,
but that evening was the only occasion when true danger,
fast, instinctive danger, seemed present. It was indeed a
strange beginning to a half-year of experiences at Kora. He
threw meat, calling to his lions.

Suddenly, one of the large cubs dashed behind George
and, as he had not seen it, I called to him softly, urgently,
'Behind you George'. The cub ran past him and George
remained unaware of the close playful antics of the young
lions which had already grown to the size of an adult leopard
and must have weighed some forty kilograms. The cub had
not attacked, but I had feared that if its antics had taken
George by surprise and if he had stumbled and fallen,
disaster would inevitably strike. The youngsters would, in all
probability, dash forward to George if he fell – a natural,
instinctive response by the young lions to a sign of weakness.
I shuddered at the thought. To underline this feeling,
suddenly, One Eye approached, head low. The lioness was
showing signs of apprehension, aggravated by the sight of the

human figures pressed against the inside of the camp fence. She was uneasy and suddenly catapulted forward, uttering deep, muttering growls. She stopped short of George, as if prompted by command or a sudden realization of the situation. She snatched the meat from the sandy ground and trotted into the bush, becoming lost to the night.

It was with a sense of relief that I watched George turn in his deliberate way and return to the small door in the camp fence. Those scenes I had witnessed impressed upon me the control, faith and strength George implanted in the lions, but also what was reflected was how the tides of time could change all too dramatically at Kora. A life's work could be dashed if, through the disability of great age, George miscalculated a lion's reactions or if he by accident stumbled to the ground while amongst the pride.

That night George was quiet. He told no stories of a lifetime of adventure, but seemed oppressed and resigned to the numbers of people sitting around his camp table consuming the nightly soup prepared by the ancient cook, Hamissi. After dinner as the others were retiring to their huts I spoke to George about our common love, lions, and of the elephants' destruction. After a short while, I bade George goodnight, pulled my stretcher out of the hut and lay down under the bright, rising moon with a scattering of images flashing in my mind. A fickle, loose breeze brushed the palm leaves on a nearby hut, playing jagged shapes across my face, and I eventually slept.

Hours later I woke suddenly and clearheaded to the deep, booming, abrupt call of George's lions. The nearest lion, probably the young male Denis, just twenty-five yards from where I lay, sounded his challenge clear and deep, permeating the still and silent camp.

Thereafter, I dozed intermittently, waking frequently to the calls of the lions who were restless, like myself, in the night. At about 4 am I suddenly heard the rumble of an approaching vehicle. The moon was still high, and such a sound at this time in the African bush is normally a foreboding of trouble.

I sat upright in the stretcher as the vehicle pulled to a halt outside the camp and human voices, high-pitched and excited, cleared my mind. Minutes later the tracker Mohammed approached from the darkness and said, 'Game department are here. There is big trouble. *Shifta* have killed two rangers and these men have found a wounded man – he is outside.'

Mohammed left me to waken George. I then understood the partial cause of that uneasy, engulfing feeling I'd had the night before, and that feeling became clear, almost tangible, as I heard the story.

At approximately eight the previous morning a game department truck carrying the local warden and three rangers had been travelling towards the small, predominantly Somalian, settlement of Boka on the south-eastern border of the reserve. What the rangers did not know was that they were driving straight into a Somali *shifta* ambush. Automatic fire, possibly from the same weapons which had ended the lives of the two elephants, smashed into the vehicle. The driver was killed instantly as the windscreen shattered, and the truck careered off the road and, hitting trees and rocks, came to a halt. From two well-concealed positions, the *shifta* continued to fire a hail of bullets into the truck. It was later discovered that the *shifta* had planned to assassinate the warden, a man who had had success in seizing poached ivory. As the vehicle crashed to its stop, only two men were still alive – the warden who, blessed with luck, then vanished into the bush, and one other ranger. As fate would have it, as the final shots were fired, a bullet ricocheted off the vehicle and slammed into the ranger. He flinched and then lay still, wounded, but not mortally. He lay unmoving, partially through shock, but also through fear that the attackers would find him alive. He remained as if dead, playing possum to a deadly foe.

Then there was silence. In time the wounded ranger opened his eyes and searched, from his prone position, for signs of the attackers. Later he stumbled into the bush, his soiled green uniform loose and a tell-tale pink stain around the bullet hole in his shirt. Neither of the two men, the ranger or warden, knew of the other's survival – each presumed that all had been slain.

The wounded ranger, a brave man with a bullet lodged in the flesh of his back, then began a twenty-hour ordeal of caution and strength as he walked through the bush towards *Kampi ya Simba*. He was found by another patrol and brought to George's camp.

We were fortunate to have Andrew, the doctor, at the camp with us. In the darkness of the early morning, George, with a *kikoi* (local cotton wrap) wrapped around his waist, roused him and soon the doctor was inspecting the man's back wound. An area of flesh, the size of a large coin, had been gouged by the tumbling bullet. This man had been very lucky as, apart from the consequent heavy bruising from the impact of the bullet, Andrew established that he had narrowly escaped very serious injury.

That scene of George, the rangers, the wounded man and the story of the tragedy sobered the minds of the visitors in the camp. It had a shock effect which, added to the sight of the elephant carcasses, dismissed the preconceived impression with which they had come to Africa – the impression of a perfect, tranquil setting – an Africa imagined only by those not of the continent.

# 3

◄ ◆ ►

# The Early Days

Life at Kora returned to a sense of normality in that strangely quick way which often follows death or tragedy. The Kenyan government were shocked and enraged by the *shiftas'* cruel murder of the rangers and, because of this incident, the GSU (General Service Unit – a Kenyan para-military team) were moved into the reserve. The GSU's job was to drive all the Somalis and their livestock out of the reserve and to hunt down the killers of the rangers. Mainly because of the rangers' death, President Arap Moi decreed that a 'shoot on sight' policy with poachers would be undertaken to curb the elephant slaughter and general destabilization in Kenya. With the GSU basing themselves four kilometres from *Kampi ya Simba*, we all drew comfort from their presence.

Also at *Kampi ya Simba* were three small lion cubs, not

more than two weeks old. The cubs' mother had tragically been shot as a cattle killer. After her death, it was discovered that she was in milk and a search for the cubs was made. The three were found. Batian, the male cub, and Rafiki and Furaha, the two females, were then handed over to George.

The tiny lions were housed in a large enclosure close to George's hut and, as they grew larger, they would sleep against the fence at night, a few feet away from George's stretcher outside the hut.

Their presence revived many memories for George, and prompted many stories. Here, after an eight-year break, was the revival of a large part of his life's work and the cubs represented the past, coupled with the future. It was some thirty-three years since the legend of Elsa had been born, and her spirit, together with the spirits of the other lions in George's life, was represented in the tiny, tumbling forms of these young lions. They, in turn, reflected the life of a man devoted to wildlife who, despite his great age, remained tireless in his quest; a life which through his sparkling eyes had seen the transformation from early 'white settler' days, through the winds of change to a land inadvertently heavily dependent, economically, upon the subject of his life's work – wildlife preservation.

During those first weeks back at Kora, away from the mix of camp visitors, I would talk to George about the past. Together we would sit, he at his desk, and I on the sandy ground in his narrow room.

Here, the past became vividly alive, enhanced by the faded pictures of Joy and Elsa, of Boy and Christian and by some of his few possessions like the gun-cleaning equipment and the old Leica camera. It was the home of a man who had never been hampered by possessions or materialism. What he owned served a purpose, a role in his life, and there was no cluttering of possessions with George.

In the mid-mornings he would sit with his glass of gin and orange, almost visibly shaking himself and ridding himself of the thoughts of present tragedies and we would lose ourselves in the mists of time, in recollection and reminiscences, tinged with happiness and pain, as the stories unfolded. George's memory was clear and seemingly unaffected by the passage of time as we delved together into the unique treasure trove of memories of his sixty-five Kenyan years which covered the life of a country.

George Adamson's life began in 1906 in India. At the age of eighteen, having completed eight years of schooling in England, he sailed to Africa's most southern point, the Cape of Good Hope. Here he was due to meet his parents who planned to settle in South Africa. When the ship docked at Cape Town he received a telegram from his father. He was in Kenya, and he liked the country immensely and wanted his son to join him in the new colony. George chuckled when telling this story, adding that he received the telegram after being rowed back to the ship with a dreadful hangover after a long evening out at the Mount Nelson Hotel.

The occasion was still vividly clear in George's mind. By the time George landed at the port of Mombasa, his parents had bought a small coffee farm outside Nairobi at a place called Limuru.

Though the colony, as a British Protectorate, was only twenty-nine years old, the legend of the African lion was already deeply etched upon the country – one of the most dramatic stories being of the man-eaters of Tsavo, which told of grisly attacks which took place in what is today the Tsavo National Park.

A railway line was to be built to link Mombasa with the settlement of Nairobi. Tens of thousands of labourers were brought across from India to work upon the line when it was discovered that the locals had no inclination to work in such a manner.

Unfortunately, as the project progressed, a group of lions began to create havoc, terrorizing the railway camps and, in particular, the Indians and their women and children. Work stopped on the railway after more than one hundred Indians had been killed and eaten. It was the chief engineer, Colonel R.J. Patterson, who eventually killed the man-eaters, but not before he too almost became a statistic on several occasions! His book, *The Man-Eaters of Tsavo*, in which he describes the dreadful events, is a classic of hunting literature and, immensely popular, is still available in print today. Unfortunately though, the man-eating did not end when Patterson killed the Tsavo pride and, further up the line, to quote the Colonel, a lion had acquired ' ... an extraordinary taste for members of the railway staff ... ' even killing and eating the superintendent of police, Mr Ryall! Finally, the lion was trapped, and, after being rather macabrely displayed, was shot.

Man-eating is an obscure form of behaviour in lions as, over countless centuries, lions have learnt through deadly experience to fear man as the two are ancestral enemies. Man-eating can also be explained as a strange trait which certain lions develop and pass on to their young. Lions do not generally kill primates such as baboons for food, nor do they feed upon competing predators such as hyenas, despite the fact that they will deliberately kill them. If we humans are seen in a not dissimilar light by lions, then man-eating is a most unusual trait that periodically arises.

This tragic spate of man-eating in Tsavo could have arisen after a famished and desperate group of lions overcame their inherent fear of man and began to kill. Quickly they would have realized the vulnerability of man as a prey species.

George would invariably chuckle when recalling Patterson's endeavours, not hesitating to mention that he remembered from stories that Patterson, who had turned to professional hunting, was involved in a rather scandalous episode when a well-titled client was killed, or died mysteriously on a safari, leaving Patterson and the client's widow to continue the safari together, sharing the same tent – but that is another story.

For the first ten years in Kenya, George embarked upon a variety of jobs. He built roads and went into the transport business, but this was short-lived. His first consignment – matches – exploded, having been ignited by the friction of his vehicle upon the rugged tracks! After this adventure he decided to turn to coffee farming, but that too he found unsatisfactory. Later, he traded in goats and beeswax, but this also failed when the goats died because of the change in altitude and his African suppliers continually forgot to keep the combs for wax when gathering the much relished honey! Later he became a salesman but, like the goat and wax business, this too languished. All these occupations lacked the essence that his spirit craved. In a sense he was like a young lion moving with wanderlust to its eventual vocation; the wandering years of a nomad, learning, developing and ultimately fulfilling a nature-dictated role.

It was at this point that George, accompanied by his great friend, Nevil Baxendale, embarked upon a quest for gold. They collected equipment, staked their claims, and were rewarded by the occasional elusive tailings of the metal in their pans. Though this was not commercially a success, it was nevertheless a life George enjoyed, and an occupation he returned to.

These were the days of the eccentrics and of indulgences, of hard work and even harder play. Characters like Lord Delamere became besotted with the country and immersed themselves and their wealth into the land. Delamere grew his hair long, became a blood brother to the Masai and was the self-appointed, unofficial spokesman for the settlers. These were the infant years of the famous Muthaiga Club with its golf course, tennis court and stables – the 'Moulin Rouge of Africa' – where famous romances, and even shootings, became associated with its name. It was the centre of marvellous parties where the settlers let off steam. Amongst the riotous revelry, Lord Delamere would shoot golf balls on to the roof of the club and climb up to retrieve them, and

Karen Blixen's lover, Denys Finch-Hatton, would butt over armchairs like a bull until he eventually ended up sitting in them.

I would ask George about the equally flamboyant women of those times, who led such fascinating lives. He would tell me that, unlike their counterparts in recession-hit Britain or America, these women had many servants, so had the opportunity to fulfil themselves and explore their talents in ways uncharacteristic of the time. This is perhaps the reason that the most vivid and descriptive portrayals of those early 'white' Kenyan days are through the words, paintings and legends of those women.

George's friend, Elspeth Huxley, produced many great books about Kenya; perhaps the most superb example of settlement by the pioneers in Kenya being *The Flame Trees of Thika*. To me, though, it is the life of Karen Blixen which embraces the aspects of life and love of the era. Hers was a life of high drama, of fatalism as her life flowed from its blossoming as a young socialite to a beautiful bride arriving at Mombasa, to a wife in a betrayed marriage and her realization of the frontiers of love discovered in a country, like herself, made of optimism, balanced precariously with pessimism. Her lover, Denys Finch-Hatton, a sensitive individualist, was a superb hunter of game and one of the pioneers of flying in Kenya; a man who, perhaps ironically, met his death in the discovered love of the freedom of flying joyously over the majestic land.

Another pioneer of Kenya's flying days of the 20s and 30s was Beryl Markham, whom George had also known. She had grown up bare-footed and uninhibited with the Nandi people. In an eventful and long life she took to flying and became the first woman mail pilot – and then the first woman to attempt a marathon east to west solo flight across the Atlantic.

The Kenya of George's younger days also received a Royal visit. The Prince of Wales, later King Edward VIII, sampled the Kenyan life and was entertained by, amongst others, Beryl Markham, Karen Blixen, her husband, Bror Blixen, and her lover, Finch-Hatton. The prince found the country delightful, a pleasurable playground which reflected his own personal tastes.

His visit, though, was brought to an abrupt end when his father, King George V, was thought to be dying. A strange coincidence is that his niece, then the Princess Elizabeth, ended her tour of Kenya, some twenty-five years later, on a similar note, with the death of her father, King George VI.

George told me that as a young man growing up in the Kenya of those times he had begun to develop a taste for hunting and his earliest expeditions took place with his brother, Terence, their transport often being only a motor cycle and sidecar. The two brothers would share a single rifle and the expense of bullets dictated that a shot must kill, and that accuracy was crucial!

George learned the language of the wilds, the sounds and signs, a learning which continued to serve him. If money was really short, the brothers would save £25 to buy an elephant licence, and then set off to kill a tusker – later selling the ivory for perhaps £50 and, on exceptional occasions, for £100. It was also during this period that George, accompanied by his companion, Baxendale, went, for the second time, in search of gold.

George always looked back fondly on this expedition, a search for the fabled Queen of Sheba's mines, which the stories of old held existed on the shores of Lake Turkana, a remote and vast stretch of water in northern Kenya. They found little gold, but the experience of freedom, adventure and the excitement of anticipation was priceless to George.

For a time he then became a professional hunter and guide, before joining the Kenyan game department in its earliest days. George was posted to Isiolo on the southern boundary of the Northern Frontier Province. The region under his guardianship was remote, harsh and vast, the size of Great Britain, and his only transport was camels, pack donkey and one small pickup.

While George, for years, led a somewhat isolated existence in the remote northern country, the immortalized antics of the Happy Valley set, with its combination of sex, drink, drugs and dangerous liaisons reached their nadir with the murder of Lord Erroll. The seductive fascist's reputation as a womanizer and philanderer became legend in the colony, and the events leading to his murder at a cross-roads outside Nairobi have, of course, been recounted fully in the book and film, *White Mischief* – works which capture the life of those times.

It was after this scandal that George met and, after some time, married Joy. I never probed him on these times, letting him volunteer occasional comment upon their lives together and apart. What many people fail to recognize is that for twenty years George and Joy Adamson experienced a mutually benefiting life together. They lived mostly on safari in northern Kenya, surrounded by the remarkable scenery the wild area offered, and together shared learning and discovery.

She was an artist capturing the scenes around her, developing her talent, while George sought after poachers and lived through the dangers of a warden's job. Together they shared a remarkable life and the essence of their love remained unbroken.

They experienced a relationship still partly veiled, a relationship between two very different personalities, but they shared common bonds. Much later in the marriage, George's devotion to his lions undoubtedly angered Joy. He chose to live in the wild with his big cats instead of living in their house together on Lake Naivasha. She perhaps felt a sense of failure. Joy was immensely talented, acclaimed as an artist and author, and an extraordinary spokeswoman for the preservation of Africa's wildlife. Partly because of this success, a shadow was cast on the fact that she still had not found complete happiness in marriage and, I feel, that she could never accept. But, despite their subsequent separate lives, one must remember that deep down, away from the probing eyes of outsiders, a private, special love existed.

It was a turbulent marriage perhaps, but Kenya too, with the incompatibility of a new black self-awareness and established colonial ways was in the 1950s about to produce the most bloody and violent period of its history.

George's accounts of this time were passive and, characteristically, recalled more the humorous aspects which arose during the country's crisis. The Mau-Mau rebels had begun their struggle to rid Kenya of colonial rule and when the emergency was declared George entered the army services, training patrols and utilizing his intricate knowledge of the bush deep within the forests of the Aberdare mountains. He rarely spoke about the horrors, perhaps because he felt it was old history and times had changed, but at the time, fearful and loathsome Kikuyu oaths to kill and drive the white man from Kenya had begun and ignited a war of four long years, a war of terrorism, troops, dive bombers and cruel murders.

The killings accounted for the lives of twenty-six Asians, ninety Europeans, one thousand eight hundred 'loyal' Africans and some eleven thousand five hundred African terrorists. This 'Mau-Mau emergency', as the British called it, was one of the first African wars of revolt against the colonial powers and, ironically, the only one Europeans were to win anywhere in Africa for two decades.

Once when talking to George about this time, I asked about the writings of Robert Ruark and his famous book, *Uhuru*. In the book, Ruark depicted people, white and black, caught up in the uncertainty of pre-independence Kenya. The story portrayed the fears of some and hopes of others for the future, vividly evoking the feeling of Kenya and its people at that time. George would repeatedly say that the poignant statement the book made for the continent's future, and the white man's future in it, were excellent. Ruark had stayed with George on safari, and it was clear that he admired the man for his writing and for the person he was. George had seen much death and many atrocities, and clearly felt that the scenes of the oath-taking, the killings in the forests, and the appalling loss of life described in Ruark's books could not have been depicted more accurately or vividly – this horror had happened. Though the Kikuyu had lost a war, they had nevertheless received a psychological boost. They had stood up to the white man and the ripples from the winds of change were to spread throughout the continent. At this time of the country's unsettled situation, an abrupt and unexpected change was about to enter George's life – a lioness called Elsa, and the phenomenon of Joy's *Born Free*. This was an important time which I will cover in more detail later in this book.

These talks I had with George would often be continued in the evenings when the other people in camp had gone to sleep, and it was in those first few weeks that I began to understand George and his life more fully.

George had people around him almost continually, and constantly had to be aware of visitors while he was perhaps never happier than when fiddling in the workshop alone or repairing some equipment in a quiet camp. I found it stressful to see George forcing himself to adapt daily to new visitors. If only George could have been allowed to enjoy people's company when it suited him. After all, George enjoyed the presence of people, being a congenial person, but he should not have been pressurized by an unending influx of visitors.

George's need for privacy reminds me of a poignant quote from Peter Matthiessen's book *The Tree Where Man Was Born*. On safari, many years ago, he and a companion saw George and his old tracker on the Samburu plains and he wrote, 'Adrian waved to the figure in the chair, who did not wave back; white man and black, at right angles to each other, remained motionless as if cast in stone. Like old buffalo these old men, like their solitude, gazing out over Africa that was.'

I would feel uncomfortable sensing the unnecessary strain on George. I knew only too well how a number of people living in close contact within a small community in the bush was a formula for problems. I have seen these bush politics many times in Botswana, and it is indeed an unnecessary problem, especially for a man merely wanting to live his last years in peace.

In those early weeks I concentrated on learning from George and wrote notes with, subconsciously, a book of this nature in mind. I hoped though that the influx of visitors and hangers-on was a passing phase, perhaps coinciding with the peak of the tourist season. But, as time went by, I began to realize that this is largely how camp life was at Kora. My role with George was to return and, for an indefinite period, neither of us making any kind of commitment, to assist him with, amongst many things, his rehabilitation project. But on my arrival, I found the three cubs being suffocated with pampering love and attendance from other people in camp, and, as one group of surrogate mothers left, another would automatically fill the vacuum – possessively, and perhaps purely for the satisfaction of their own egos. Their attention and time with the cubs forced even George to be distanced from his little ones. Despite this sad situation the tiny cubs, though initially having dehydration problems, were well. They spent most of their time in the shade of a wooden structure in the enclosure, attempting to escape the heat of the days.

I would accompany George on searches for Growe's pride of eight and, most of all, observe life within the camp and outside in the reserve. I learned, and read up on, the area and its facets, and it was not long before I realized what a truly wonderful wilderness area Kora is. Its recent history is one undeniably merged with man. The dhow trade across the Indian Ocean and to the States of the Gulf is an ancient one.

Some of the most sought-after goods to be transported were frankincense and myrrh, which were gathered in areas like Kora. I learned from George that the myrrh is derived from the commiphora tree and the frankincense from the *Boswellia carteri*, the families being closely related.

A major feature of Kora is the Tana River, fed by streams from the southern and eastern slopes of Mount Kenya and the eastern slope of the Aberdares. Today it flows murkily through a series of dams, where once it was a clear, clean river pulsating, unimpeded, to the Indian Ocean.

When I arrived in the region its banks were grazed bare by the undiscriminating herds of the Somali, and the hippopotamus population, having just recovered from the effects of a previous drought, was facing a yet more disastrous future. Many of the finger-splayed doum palm trees had been destroyed by the same livestock herders burning the land in a desperate attempt to encourage new growth. But the stillness, and seemingly dying appearance of Kora, is deceiving, as it is a harsh land, and in Africa these areas can transform rapidly if conditions become optimum. Kora, as a wilderness, is unique, but to most people, unfortunately, it does not have the aesthetically pleasing appearance of say the Masai Mara or Amboseli Reserves. It is, though, the type of country I enjoy. The dryness, low rainfall, and elusive animal inhabitants all combine to create the mystique of true wilderness.

In 1970, just a hundred years after the early European explorers had pushed into the thorny tangle of Njika, George came to settle in this region which was, through his presence, later to become the Kora National Reserve. George had come to this area to continue his work and to seek refuge and rehabilitation for the lion, 'Christian', and those that followed. The area was seemingly ideal, as this triangle of dense acacia/commiphora bush seemed to be a protected enclave between the agriculturalist to the west and the pastoralist in the south and east.

George had first been in the Kora area many years before

and remembered the thick bush, the isolation and the possible safe haven it could become for him and his lions. He was accompanied by his brother Terence, who had spent years working throughout Kenya on road construction. His skill was much needed if a proper road infrastructure was to be developed within this region.

They chose a site beneath the dramatic Kora Rock and Kora 'tit', as it later became known, to position *Kampi ya Simba*. These two massive rocks have a protective and seemingly calming presence and, uncannily, the images of lions are upon them.

On moonlit nights I could see on the sheer cliff of Kora Rock the huge regal face of a male lion, while upon the side the vivid image of a lioness, mouth agape, could be made out. Strangely, in certain light, other leonine shapes are discernible. It seemed more than chance that brought George to Kora to find his final home with his lions among the rocks and their time-etched tawny shapes. Kora is appropriately named, for in the local Orma language, Kora means 'the meeting place' – the place where, in the past, warriors would gather before launching attacks upon neighbouring tribes.

By 1970, the first roads were cut by the local people led by Terence. Mohammed, the tracker, told me of the many times when the teams would suddenly scatter, ant-like, into the bush when cutting the tracks.

The region then was inhabited by many black rhino, and inadvertently the road crews and a rhino would meet to the consternation of both! The men would tear away from the approaching chuffing sound of an irate rhino, while Terence would be shouting in an attempt to call his workers back.

Such scenes were indeed that of the past and would not occur today, simply because the rhinos no longer exist. As with the elephant and its ivory, the rhino is cursed by its horn which commands such a high price in the Middle East. Poachers, George told me, slaughtered every single rhino in Kora and not one was left.

# 4

◄ ◆ ►

# Kora Life and
# a Lion Called Lucifer

Today, Kora is still isolated in Kenyan terms, far from stores or the basic facilities of a conventional telephone or electricity. At camp, the only means of communication to the outside world is a radio telephone which, amidst the crackles of the usually poor reception, links *Kampi ya Simba* to the main telephone system. The radio telephone is vitally important, especially if illness or accident arises. Through the radio telephone, the Flying Doctor service in Nairobi can be contacted and a plane with trained medical staff can reach Kora within an hour or so.

Whenever supplies or fuel, or both, ran short, a trip to the nearest sizeable town, Mwingi, would be organized. Mwingi was over four and a half hours' drive from camp, a journey which always involved a drama or two, and at the very least entailed a puncture, or a minor breakdown.

Early in the morning the staff would load one of the Land Rovers with empty forty-four gallon petrol drums and crates of empty bottles and would tie them all down securely with sisal rope, knowing only too well how the rutted, corrugated roads could rattle loose any load which had the slightest slack in its mooring.

On the mornings when I did a 'Mwingi trip', I would check the vehicle for adequate fuel, oil and water, make sure that the jack, tyre lever, pump and anything else which would be essential to solving a mechanical emergency in the bush, were behind the seat, along with five litres of emergency water for the vehicle and, of course, for us embarking upon the trip. I would then clamber into the Land Rover, usually accompanied by a camp visitor, wave goodbye to George and drive out of the camp with Mohammed or one of the other staff seated upon the load in the open back of the vehicle.

These journeys were always of interest, as they entailed driving south through the reserve and into the Kitui Reserve before reaching the Shamba country beyond. Game is shy in Kora and, partly because of low visibility in the dense bush, is only occasionally sighted. To me, though, each sighting was rewarding, perhaps more so than witnessing masses of herds in other parts of Kenya.

Kora is part of a fascinating ecosystem, a Nyika* wilderness, and though the area does not have the visual appeal of other East African reserves, it nevertheless represents an area in dire need of protection. Its components and harsh habitat types are a wonder house of adaptation and, hidden, is a treasure trove of facts which could be added

---

* Nyika – Old East African term for wild, isolated country. Today a term used by scientists when referring to such regions.

to our limited library of knowledge of such existing regions. If we knew more about Kora the facts would then contribute towards producing conservation management guidelines to be applied not only in Kora but in other similar areas in Africa.

On the drive through the reserve, lesser kudu, slighter and more attractive than their cousin, the greater kudu, might dart across the road, and if I were lucky, a gerenuk, those long-necked true inhabitants of this arid land, might be seen. Gerenuk are medium-sized antelope, roughly the size of an impala, of similar colouring, but they have an elongated neck which enables them to reach higher browse. They also launch themselves on to their hind legs and feed, much like desperate goats in a drought-stricken land.

During these drives I would keep an eye open for any sign of elephants, and was only occasionally rewarded by the circular tread marks, and usually these were of young elephants wandering alone, or in small groups. Such signs are proof of the severe elephant slaughter which has taken place over the recent years in Kora. If only young elephants are encountered, it means that the adult population must have been hunted extensively.

Within the highly developed social system of elephants, this kind of situation spells disaster; it signals the collapse of the social structure. The slaughter of the old cows which govern the matriarchal society results in leaderless families and confused groups of orphaned calves. Through these killings, the survivors have lost their knowledge of the area and its resources. The slaughtered matriarchs held wisdom of long years – of avoidance of dangerous situations and the experience of knowing where food and water could be sought in dry periods. The decline of elephants within an area such as Kora has further far-reaching repercussions, as the elephants are a lynchpin in the ecosystem. The elephants' role is to open up the thick acacia/commiphora woodlands, allowing grasslands to develop and thus, inadvertently, they create feeding grounds for grazers such as eland, zebra and

other antelope. With a stable elephant population within the
region, grassland can spread and, in turn, the water table
rises as the roots of perennial grasses break up the hard
ground created by permanent scrubby bush.

Often upon these journeys I would ponder on what,
long-term, would occur at Kora without the work of these
wonderful bush architects – the elephant herds. Certainly
without the elephants, the bush will become even more
dense and less desirable for the grazing species. In a natural
balance, elephants destroy trees, but also create life.
Elephants are carriers of seed, providing ample browse for
the leaf-eaters in years to come. With the disappearance of
elephants, the less desirable scrub will close in, seasonal
streams will dry up and waterholes created by tusking and
mud-wallowing will disappear, along with Africa's oldest
roads, the elephant trails.

Indeed there is much work to be done to stop the
continuance of imbalance which, in years to come, could
bring about ecological disaster to which, man, with his
numbers of livestock, has greatly contributed. The remaining
Kora elephants have to be protected and, for that possibility,
in those first weeks at Kora, I had hope – a hope which
developed as a hard shell in my mind to counter the ultimate
pessimism and possible acceptance of the course of things.
Kora is merely a National Reserve, run by the local county
council and, because of its 'reserve' status, it does not have
the security or protection of the National Parks which are
totally the government's concern.

The southern border of the Kora Reserve and the
adjoining northern border of the Kitui Reserve is a long,
overgrown cutline hacked through the bush years ago by
Terence's teams. It is the dividing point of two reserves.
Sadly, though, because of the lack of funds, inadequate
equipment and staff, these areas have been left to the mercy
of the Somali with their herds and the ivory poachers with
their guns. Indeed, the fact that Kora had marginal

protection was merely because of the presence of George. The world-wide interest in his work with lions and the attention it focused and, because the local people were deriving income through George's presence, meant that Kora was officially gazetted a National Game Reserve on 19 October 1973. Without him, I believe it would have become yet another forgotten land.

As I drove through those scrub lands plans, proven and working in other parts of Africa, would come to mind. Today, the ultimate future of such areas of wilderness depends upon the inhabitants surrounding the reserves, and if they are directly gaining from the area, then the reserve's survival is ensured. Within Kora many projects could, with perseverance, be developed; the first being the training and creation of employment for local inhabitants. Kora could never be an area of high tourism, but a more selective form of tourism could be introduced – a form which incorporates the components of Kora as a wilderness.

One of my early ideas for Kora, which I discussed with George, was to introduce the concept of wilderness trails, where small groups of enthusiasts would be taken into the bush country to discover and explore the area. Emphasis would be upon the facets which make up the region – the trees, the *inselbergs* and the life that the area supports. Nights would be spent in rustic wilderness camps around a bright fire listening to the noises of the night, like the lyrical call of pearl-spotted owls, and the distant rumble of the lions. This kind of wilderness experience is today becoming increasingly popular in southern Africa, as it gives the city dweller the opportunity to escape from the tangle of life in that human jungle to his animal roots in Africa's last wilderness. Today, I feel, through being involved in wildlife for seven years, people are now searching for an alternative to game viewing from vehicles, and seek the spiritual awakening of a closer kinship with the bush.

One only has to look at how people have changed from an

initial interest in wild animals and bird life to an interest in the wilderness' major components – the life chains, the trees and the land itself. The establishing of such trails at Kora would produce training programmes for trackers like Mohammed, who have great initiative in the bush, and who have the potential to become competent trail officers, and who would be a delight to the trailist. Camp staff would also be needed in such an operation. Trails would generate money and job opportunities, and a cornerstone would be built which would show outsiders that, if for nothing else, Kora is worth preserving as a contributing viable financial venture. But those were just developing ideas to which I added in the months to come.

After driving through the Kitui Reserve, *shambas* (farms) would suddenly appear and, once again, the sinking feeling of being back in the world of man and villages would surface. On most occasions we would stop off at the game ranger's headquarters to hear any news of *shifta* and to check if the rangers required any provisions from the town of Mwingi.

From there I would continue towards the small town of Kyso. Along the way people were nearly always evident, emphasizing once again the great population growth that Kenya has – the largest in Africa.

At Kyso it was customary to stop at the Catholic Mission to see Father Jerry, a wonderful Irish extrovert, whose chat and hospitality were always treasured. Jerry had been in Kenya for some years, and as I grew to know him, I realized the passion the man had for the people around him. He spoke the local language fluently, and had delved into the customs and traditions of the local people. He did not, as did many other missionaries, over-implant foreign ways upon the people, believing that a combination results in the best receptiveness to religion and his missionary work. It was one of my biggest regrets that I did not get to know more of Jerry's work as he was a staunch supporter of 'his' people, and was often outspoken in his outlook.

*Kampi ya Simba* from the air.

With George Adamson in the mess hut *(Jane Hunter)*.

Denis looks out as the rest of Growe's pride feeds.

With one of Growe's youngsters *(Carla)*.

George bottle-feeds two cubs at Kora, December 1988 (*Jane Hunter*).

Rafiki — one of the orphaned cubs in George's care.

Growe — 'the Lions Legacy'.

Playing with Batian *(Julie Marshall)*.

With the Adamson lions in transit at the Nairobi National Park *(Joe Cheffings)*.

Two of the cubs on a rock at Kora *(Jane Hunter)*.

George with one of the tiny cubs.

Mohammed Maru, one
of George's lion men.

Hamissi working in the 'kitchen corner'
of *Kampi ya Simba*.

Jerry lived in a cottage framed by blossoming bougain-villaea. He was in his thirties and had a face that was a true product of his strong Irish roots. He was also a marvellous musician, another facet that endeared him to the local community, and he was a worthy soccer player!

This unorthodox missionary, who played football with the schoolchildren, was a close friend of Tony Fitzjohn, and I greatly appreciated his acceptance of my presence at Kora. Tony's long years at Kora would always be remembered fondly by Jerry, but he did not dwell on the past – he looked ahead, and embraced with enthusiasm the new hopes and plans an outsider could bring to the reserve.

After a jovial stop-off with Jerry, the Mwingi trip would continue for an hour and a half and, once reaching the town, the rush of buying and loading provisions would begin. Mwingi has little charm. It is a mixture of traditional Africa, with a colourful market, and the intrusion of modern buildings and crumbling older colonial sites, which certainly were not compatible. Mwingi was functional. Nothing more and nothing less. It was a place where fuel, gas and food, the backbone of projects at Kora, could be obtained and where a mailbox bursting with letters from all over the world would be waiting.

Usually we would lunch in one of the small restaurants, feeding hungrily off boiled rice, chapaties and eggs. Mwingi was a place to get into and out of as quickly as possible for many reasons – one being that the much slower, loaded trip back to Kora still had to be negotiated.

The journey back would normally find us at sunset, on the cutline of the reserve, whereupon a couple of warm beers would be extracted from the crates and, for a while, Mohammed and I would relax in the tranquil quietness of the bush before pushing on for the last hour to the camp.

A drive through Kora at night was always filled with surprises. Occasionally the eyes of a striped hyena would reflect, like diamonds, in the Land Rover's headlights, and at other times a herd of giraffe would be seen silhouetted in the moonlight. Bush babies would spring from branch to branch, and bat-eared fox families would rush ahead of the light, the fur on their brush-like tails standing erect, in alarm.

Eventually, barring any major vehicle problems, we would rumble into camp (some eleven hours after leaving) to the greeting of the staff and George, who would meet our arrival with 'Safe journey ...? Well, I'm sure you need a drink now ... '

Leaving the staff to unload, I would enter the cubs' enclosure to enjoy their riotous greeting, then I would wearily slump down in a chair at the drinks table.

The aftermath of these journeys always made one feel as if a mini-expedition had been completed. And it was on the return from one of these trips that something happened which challenged me to a difficult task which was to last some three months.

One day, Sue Gardner – an English friend of George's and Tony's – and I, were returning late in the afternoon from a Mwingi trip, and we were both tired from the long journey. We passed the game department camp on the edge of the Kitui National Reserve, and I slowed down to wave at the rangers sitting outside. Suddenly a uniform-clad figure burst from the main building, shouting and gesturing at me to stop. Mohammed, who was sitting on the back of the Land Rover, saw the man making all these overtures to us, and started to bang on the roof.

Thinking the worst, I braked – perhaps there had been a *shifta* attack, or poachers had struck again. But, as the man approached, I saw that he was grinning widely, and all such negative thoughts left me. It was the cheerful game department sergeant, and Mohammed leapt to the ground to meet him. The two men then began an animated conversation – the only words I could understand being, '*Mbili Simba* ... collar.... ' I thought to myself, surely they were not talking about Lucifer, the lion who had disappeared some months ago and was long presumed dead?

Lucifer's story is a fascinating one and began three years before when he and a litter mate were found near Tony Fitzjohn's camp (which was about fourteen kilometres from *Kampi ya Simba*). The one cub lay motionless, already dead, while the other tried desperately to hide when confronted by humans for the first time in its short life. The young lion cub was caught and, on seeing its condition, Tony and Kim were doubtful as to whether the little male would survive. It was only about two weeks old, and was severely dehydrated. There was no sign of the mother – perhaps she, too, was dead or, as is often the case with a lioness' first litter, she had simply abandoned the cubs. For the next few days, Tony and Kim patiently nursed the little cub which was so seriously ill that at one time it was placed on a drip by a vet who feared that the severe dehydration would take its life.

George was delighted that the cub had been found, and in retrospect, I feel that he would have dearly liked to rear the cub himself. Lucifer was a survivor and, under the care of Tony, Kim and Mohammed, he grew into a fine young lion and later shared an unusual relationship with Tony's rehabilitated leopard, Komunyu. The two would wander through the bush together and would play as though they were of the same species, instead of the enemies lions and leopards naturally are.

It was hoped that one day George's pride of Growe and the others would accept the young lions, but this was not to be. He was attacked on several occasions, and was badly bitten. The pride were also associating with a wild adult male, and there was little chance that Lucifer would ever be able to assert himself against such a foe. For long periods he had to remain, for his own safety, inside a wire enclosure. Mohammed spent much time with this lion, and undoubtedly there was a strong bond between them. He developed a great affection for Lucifer.

Finally, Lucifer, at the age of about two years,

disappeared. He had begun to wander widely and, though he had a radio collar around his neck, it was not easy to keep in contact with his movements – signals became erratic and faint. Finally no more signals were heard from the transmitter and, after many searches, including aerial reconnoitring, it was presumed that he was dead – perhaps, if he had been preying upon Somali livestock, slain by retaliating herders.

That evening I saw the delight on Mohammed's face, as he turned to me and said, 'The sergeant saw a lion with a collar, and a female at the drum on the cutline. This is Lucifer, I am sure.' Sue was also delighted at the news as, on previous visits to George and Tony, she had grown to love this lion which had been spurned by his own kind. I told Mohammed to ask again when and where the sergeant had seen the lions, to which the reply was, 'Yesterday in the late afternoon and by the rusting drum on the main road to camp....'

We thanked the sergeant and drove off, heading in the direction the lion had been seen. We half expected to come across him upon the sandy track before us, but I knew that rarely do such things come so easily in the bush.

Much later, when the sun had set, Mohammed tapped on the Land Rover's roof, signalling me to stop. We had reached the drum and we stepped from the vehicle to search for tracks in the Land Rover's lights. Amazingly, within inches of where I had braked, were the sizeable tracks of a young male lion, and nearby the particularly small tracks of a female. Mohammed stared for some seconds at the tracks, before raising his head with a smile and saying, 'Look, this Lucifer – see here.' He indicated a slight scuff on the track of the lion's hind foot. 'Somali wounded him with a spear and see, he walks like this ... ' He turned his hand, curling his fingers inward like claws, and then twisted the hand into the sand.

I then remembered how George had mentioned that the lion had received a severe spear wound from Somalis and this had caused him to walk with a slight limp, which left a track with a scuff as a trademark. His tracks could never be mistaken.

We continued back to camp, driving slowly through the night, hoping to chance upon the reflection of a lion's amber eyes. We arrived late, but there was George, as always, to meet the vehicle. Sue jumped from the Land Rover and excitedly said, 'George, Lucifer is alive!' George turned to me quizzically for an explanation, and I told him the story. Later that night, in confirmation of the events, I called Mohammed from the staff quarters to give the exciting story in his way.

George was happy with the news but knew, as I did, that if the lion was Lucifer, his collar would have become exceedingly tight and would have to be removed. Lucifer had disappeared at the age of two, and in the past year his body would have developed rapidly – becoming bulkier as he reached prime.

George later confided that there were vague rumours that a young male lion had, some months before, leapt upon a sleeping man at the village of Boka and had also killed several donkeys. There was no proof that it was Lucifer, but it was worrying that there were even suspicions as to who the lion was. Also, if Lucifer was killing stock, the blame would be visited upon George and the repercussions could affect the current project – the future of the new cubs. Lucifer had to be tracked and found. In doing this, apart from removing his collar, we would learn about his movements and whether he really was a threat to livestock.

The following morning I drove to where I had seen the tracks the day before, and followed them until both sets disappeared deep into a section of impenetrable thorn country. I returned to camp and discussed with George how we should go about finding the lion. At the time, I did not know that part of Kora and I pondered over the maps, puzzling with George over the likely areas Lucifer could be and discussing where, in that waterless tract, the lion could possibly be drinking.

That evening began weeks of similar searches for the elusive Lucifer, 'the devil in darkness' as I later called him. Sue and I left camp after George and I had planned how we would try to find this lion. We took a mattress to sleep on the roof of George's oldest vehicle, the 'Nightingale', some food, water, torches and most important of all, a rifle – George's ancient game department issue, a .303 – and the loud hailer.

In recent years George had used a loud hailer to attract his lions to the camp or his vehicle. This worked more effectively and over greater distances than merely shouting for them. George felt that, despite the time lapse since he had had contact with Lucifer, the lion would still respond to the sound of his name being called through the loud hailer.

The initial plan was to drive to 'Lucifer's drum' as the rusting forty-four gallon petrol drum became known, and to wait through the night to see whether he would be attracted by the calls I would make. That night, Sue and I alternately did two-hour shifts, sharing the long night watch. I called through the loud hailer, 'Come on Lucifer. Come on,' and my voice would echo, then become lost in the African night. In the weeks ahead, despite the punishingly hot days and little sleep, I never became blasé about the beauty of an African night. I always enjoyed each time, lying down and peering up into the magical sky, following the progress of satellites and counting the numbers of shooting stars.

The nights were always filled with expectancy, with potential drama, and yet calmness of spirit prevailed, and this was how the first 'Lucifer night' was.

During my watches, I listened intently for any low calls, the padding of paws upon the still ground, but there were none. At dawn we stretched and climbed down from the Land Rover to minutely inspect the road and surrounds for tracks. There was only the pinched-toed trail of a passing jackal, and further up the road, the tracks of a striped hyena. The doves had already begun the maniacal circles upon the ground and I decided to drive slowly back to camp still searching for signs of the lion.

After making a small fire to boil water for tea, and having repacked the vehicle, we set off slowly down the track towards Kora, some forty kilometres away. I had only driven seven kilometres before, across the road, I spied the tracks of a lion. I slammed on the brakes and leapt out excitedly. There was no mistake – it was the same spoor – the same scuffed track, and it was fresh, perhaps only an hour or so old.

I told Sue the news then, parking the Land Rover off the road, instructed her on what we were about to do. Following up lions on foot in the African bush has certain ground rules – you never walk in front of the person tracking, and who has the rifle, stand behind him always, and never, when the lion has been seen, show any fear. Lastly, if the lion rushes forward in a charge (most of which are mock) never run, stand your ground.

All this I told Sue, but I also asked her, at intervals, to drag a stick behind her in stony or thick ground so that, in the particularly bad country, we would have an indication of the direction we had come from. As a rule I do not like taking unbush-trained people on foot after lion. It is a daunting responsibility, and the constant watchfulness for the safety of others detracts from the concentration needed to interpret signs and spoor. Too much can go wrong when you are accompanied by those who are not as bush-oriented as necessary.

When tracking lions people become completely unpredictable. Despite assurances before setting off, when a situation becomes dangerous, people don't control their actions – a sense of pure self-preservation takes over, and this is a sure-fire recipe for disaster.

We left the vehicle and, for an hour and a half, and as the

sun moved higher into the sky, I followed the lion spoor. I stopped at times to peer at the sun, hoping that by now its blasting rays would draw the lion into shadow, and to slumber, but this lion continued to head to a seemingly predestined point. Finally, I left the spoor when it crossed a deep gulley. There were none of the usual signs that he might stop, signs such as finding the imprint of his body upon the ground where he had rested for a short while, or the heading of the spoor into deep undergrowth where he might lie up for the day.

I decided to return to the same point that evening, and again I would wait up and call for him. Sue and I travelled the hour-long journey back to camp and, back in the mess hut, George was delighted with the information I had gathered, and encouraged me to continue the search for Lucifer.

That evening, Sue and I returned at sunset to the drum, and again, at intervals, I called through the loud hailer. That night we had visits from two cats. I had just fallen asleep when Sue woke me saying that she had heard an animal walking nearby. Tired, and a little irritable, I shone the spotlight and saw nothing. Later, I clambered down from the Land Rover roof and scanned the ground. The light fell upon the fresh tracks of a male leopard. He had approached the vehicle, stopped within four paces, then walked in a half circle around us and into the night. It made me wonder whether it was the male leopard, Attila, which Tony had released some years before, and which had never been seen again. This was exceedingly unlikely, but it was an unusual course of events. An even stranger one was about to take place.

Hours later, with Sue asleep, I crept down from the vehicle. There was a faint glow of the false dawn in the sky and I was impatient to discover if there were any signs of the lion on the road. Still using the torch, I searched for spoor. In the light a reflection caught my eye and, to my surprise, I found tatters of clothing, and examined my find. It was clear that the items had been lying there for many months, but a tingly feeling of George's account of a young male lion's suspected attack came to mind.

As I crouched, I suddenly heard the sound of an animal brushing against the undergrowth, some twenty yards away. I kept still and listened. It could just have been a kudu or gerenuk that had sensed my presence, but deep inside me, I felt it was much more. I then shone the torch in the direction of the sounds but saw nothing but vegetation. Slowly, I stood and walked back to the vehicle. I left Sue to sleep until the sun broke over the horizon and lit the birth of a new day. I prepared a fire and set the pot to boil water, at the same time eager to return to where I had heard the sounds in the darkness.

With tea ready, I woke Sue and told her of what had happened an hour or so before. Together we walked along the road, my senses heightened with expectation. There they were, fresh lion tracks, and definitely again those of Lucifer. Slowly, I pieced together what had happened in those hours of darkness. He had been walking towards the Land Rover along the track. On the dust I back-tracked his spoor for over a hundred yards. In the darkness, he had seen me, then turned, seemingly crouching beneath a bush on the road's verge, and there he had watched as I, some thirty yards away, crouched over the tatters of clothing. Then he had left the track and walked in a broad avoiding circle some distance from the vehicle and disappeared – the sounds of his body pushing through the undergrowth being what I had heard as he left the track.

Had he come deliberately or not, was the tantalizing question. Had he responded to my call? To continue tracking him was difficult as it was as if he had, with deliberation, chosen the most difficult and unfavourable route to track a lion – through thorny, dense terrain. Nevertheless, we tried to follow his tracks, but the thorn and our slow pace made the task fruitless. He would, by now, be far away.

As the days passed, so the tantalizing glimpses of Lucifer's life unfolded to me. I explored the dry riverbeds where he walked, using them as avenues of easy access through the dense bush. I found that at that time of year there was no surface water and that Lucifer must survive for months without drinking. There was no indication that he moved down to the Tana river, some twenty-five kilometres from what seemed to be his 'core' area, the area in which he spent much of his time. This was a particularly interesting observation, as it is similar to the findings of researchers in the Kalahari Desert where it was discovered that lions were not dependent upon water and will drink only when it is available. So, like lions in the Kalahari, it did not seem that water determined Lucifer's movements. In such dry regions, lions satisfy their liquid requirements from the prey they eat, though, in the Kalahari, it was also observed that lions would, on occasion, eat the moisture-filled tsama melons and nama fruits.

I also found no evidence of Lucifer's kills. This indicated that large prey were low in number and that he must be killing smaller prey such as gerenuk. From such kills very little would remain and, after the scavengers like jackal and striped hyena had scattered the remains, in a very short period of time, virtually no signs of the kill would be evident.

I grew to know the country fairly well and, despite its thorny and hostile appearance, in time I loved this land in which a lion, born in the wilds, raised by man, rejected by his own kind, had eventually made his home. It was also, at this point, that George introduced me to the art of divining as an added means of determining Lucifer's whereabouts.

I had an open mind about such a phenomenon, and after talking with George, I was sufficiently intrigued to attempt to use his brother's technique.

Terence had passed away two years previously at Kora,

but up to the time of his death, he used his gift of divining regularly. He could search for just about anything, including George's lions. I heard tell, on occasions, how Terence's success rate was comparable to the time-consuming task of following up on the lion's tracks, and preferable to radio tracking. Terence's technique of divining, I learned, entailed using a pendulum on a string, a map, a pencil and a photograph of a lion. Terence would concentrate upon the photograph as he dangled the pendulum over a map of Kora, and would pinpoint the lion's position when the weight began to circle over a particular area. Also, somewhat strangely, if the pendulum swung in a clockwise direction, it indicated that the lion was alive while anti-clockwise movement indicated death. Terence's gift was remarkable as he divined successfully for water, geological faults and, on one occasion, even indicated to a woman where her lost son was to be found!

I used Terence's pendulum frequently in the first three weeks of searching for Lucifer. On occasions, the results were fairly good, but they were not consistent. The pendulum would indicate an area to me at times and I would find Lucifer's tracks when reaching the area. I did not possess Terence's gift, but I feel that a talent for such phenomena can be developed, and often wished that I had known about such matters while at the North East Tuli Block in Botswana when I wished to locate lions I had not seen for some time.

# 5

◄ ♦ ►

# Filming the 'Free' Years

After spending nearly a month searching for Lucifer, George, the staff, visitors and I began preparing the camp for the arrival of a television crew from Britain who were due at Kora to produce a documentary on George's long and eventful life. Doddie Edmonds, George's secretarial and camp assistant, was also returning to camp after a period away in Britain. Doddie is a cheerful young Englishwoman who had been with George for seven years, staying sometimes for a year and occasionally for just a few months.

Other inhabitants at this time, apart from Sue, were Carla, a young American girl who had come on vacation to visit George, and David, who had been a zoo-keeper in England, referred to George by Bill Travers after his work on exposing the bad conditions in which animals are kept in a particular zoo in Britain. Dave also assisted in the moving of six circus tigers to India. The cats are now living within an extensive enclosure in their indigenous habitat. The tigers, it was discovered, were being kept in a small, caravan-sized beast-wagon in southern England. Dave's commitment to animals was clearly genuine.

Last, but not least in camp, was Julie, a nineteen-year-old English girl who, on reading George's marvellous autobiography, *My Pride and Joy*, was so inspired by his work that for months she saved money to fly to Kenya to have the opportunity of meeting him. When, on her arrival, I saw her small physique, snow-white complexion and total ignorance of the bush, I felt that she was a most unlikely candidate to adapt to living with us for any length of time. In the months to come she was to prove me very wrong. A typical English pioneer spirit emerged, and she endured the life exceedingly well, assisting me tremendously and under difficult conditions.

I continued to search for Lucifer over the next few days. Again we got close to him, but even a brief sighting was not to be.

One evening, when I returned to camp, I discovered that part of the television team had arrived. I walked into the mess hut to introduce myself to them. The producer was Nick, an affable fellow who had a quiet air of scepticism and, I discovered, a charmingly dry sense of humour. Narrator and interviewer for the film was Sandy Gall, author and well-known television journalist and newscaster from Britain's ITN. Lastly, there was Adrian House, a man long associated with the Adamsons and a former director of Collins. Adrian had worked extensively on Joy's books and had contributed greatly to *My Pride and Joy*. His knowledge of George's life was an essential ingredient in the production of the movie.

I enjoyed meeting these men as their no-nonsense outlook and appreciation of the work which had to be done was a welcome contrast to the usual influx of visitors to camp.

That evening we chatted about plans for the days ahead and I found the discussions stimulating, as I found they also drew out my own thoughts and ideas for the project. I also sensed though that the subsequent film was to be angled as a tribute to George and his life and a necessary (though it was a morbid thought at the time) obituary to George. I wondered how he must have felt about this, for he obviously knew on what occasion the film would have its greatest impact. This kind of situation was enough to make anybody ponder privately upon his mortality.

The following day the camera and sound crew arrived from Nairobi in a hired Land Rover. The team consisted of Mike Shimpton, a tall strong cameraman whose expertise with his camera was, of course, ultimately what the film depended upon. His assistant was John who arrived, clearly excited, if not bewildered, by the unusual surroundings. Lastly, there was the sound man, Rod Louhouse, who had worked extensively both on major films and documentaries.

A few days before the arrival of the film team, Growe and her pride had disappeared and defied George's search for them. This was a major problem for the film makers. After lunch on the day of their arrival, I gathered how important it was for the pride to be found. I suggested that I postpone the search for Lucifer and that I attempt to find the pride, and soon we had spread the map of Kora on the table between us and were discussing the lions' likely whereabouts. From the talk around the table, I realized even more how important it was to locate the pride, for essential footage for the film would be scenes of George amongst his lions. Such scenes would symbolize the essence of the man and his unique situation.

In the days ahead, George worked tirelessly upon the project, exhibiting a drive which largely banished his thoughts on the present problems in the reserve. The film proved to be a great motivation for him and undeniably raised his spirits, spurring reserves of energy I had not previously seen in him.

The evening of the film crew's arrival, Sue and I set out to spend the night in the bush searching for Growe's pride. I placed a particularly old camel carcass, which was to be used as a lure for the lions, in a trailer which I attached to the Nightingale, the old Land Rover. We headed down to the murky Tana River, then drove upstream to where George had found tracks of the pride a day before. An hour before sundown, I found the lions' spoor heading up a gulley. I unloaded the carcass from the trailer, sliced through the putrefying flesh, tied a chain through the pelvis and attached the chain to the Nightingale. I was using a technique for luring lions which I had applied on occasions in Botswana; the plan being to drag the carcass to where the lions might come across its scent, inducing them to follow the trail to where we would be waiting.

With a long-handled Somali knife Mohammed had given me as a gift, I punctured the carcass to allow the gastric ooze of the stomach to seep out on to the road. This left behind a tempting lure for the lions. We drove off, pulling the bouncing carcass behind us and, after several kilometres, stopped in an open area on the banks of the Tana River and a tributary stream called the Mununi. Night fell swiftly and Sue and I unloaded the equipment from the vehicle for the night-long vigil ahead. A clear sliver of new moon pierced the sky and, unfortunately, the wind began to blow. I called, periodically, through the loud hailer, in the hope that the lions would be near. Inwardly, however, I knew that they would not visit us that night. It is the kind of feeling one develops in the bush — it's inexplicable but often accurate.

The night was long and uneventful. As the sun rose in the east, I awoke from an uncomfortable, uneasy slumber, a half-awake form of sleep which develops after long nights in the bush waiting for lions. It's a sleep which leaves one continually fatigued until a good rest, or a lion sighting, revives the body and spirit. I was impatient and eager to find the lions, but all that had visited the putrefying carcass that night were a few shifty jackals and two striped hyenas.

Sue and I packed the vehicle and she sensed my determination to find the pride. We drove down the river road and before long I found the pride's spoor. They had moved across to the stony, thorn country in the south-east, then swung north to the river to slake their thirst.

The tracks I found were fresh, recently imprinted into the soft dust. I was delighted. There were the small spoor of the cubs and the larger tracks of the young male, Denis, and I assessed the situation. The lions had drunk from this point an hour or so before, then headed inland back towards a magnificent cluster of *inselbergs* known as Kauma.

The day before, I had told George that we would return to camp by mid-morning to report our findings, but these fresh tracks tempted me on. I decided that I would follow in the wake of the lions while Sue drove to camp to report what was happening. After restocking with water, fuel and meat for the lions, she would return with Mohammed to meet me at the gulley whereupon, depending upon what I had found, we would prepare for the evening.

She drove away and I stood alone with the rifle and water container – alone but without the feeling of vulnerability that is usually associated with that state. I was delighted to have found the lions' tracks and I set out looking for the pride.

The ground was stony, which made tracking slow, but I saw they had crossed the lugga and, as I followed, I pondered as to where they might be. The sun's energy-sapping heat pounded down and soon I was soaked with sweat. I followed the lions' tracks for an hour before turning back to where I was to meet Sue. By now I knew I had an excellent chance of finding the pride that evening, judging by their direction and where I estimated they would spend their subsequent daytime slumbers.

By the time I had trekked back to the Tana River, I was experiencing the satisfying lethargy of exertion under the

African sun and, happily, this feeling was coupled by my knowledge that the lions would be found. I sat beneath a wide, spreading grove of palm trees and watched the river through slowly closing eyes, then sleep stole my senses.

I woke sometime later to the distant rumble of the returning vehicle. I stood, stretched and moved from the Tana's banks to meet Sue and Mohammed. I decided to follow the tracks in the vehicle and, an hour later, through the thorn and rock, we found ourselves parallel with the Kaume Hills. I knew that the lions were close and that almost magnetic feeling relieved and excited me and filled me with anticipation that we would be with the lions that evening. By now it was furnace hot and the lions would have stopped travelling long ago. Knowing this we drove back to camp to discuss our findings with George and the film team.

After a most welcome lunch and subsequent lively conversation it was decided that if I found the lions that evening I should stay with them. We would keep in touch with the film crew through the portable radio sets Rod was busily rigging up.

Later, Sue and I set out again – this time accompanied by Mohammed. We drove off to the Kaume Hills where we planned to spend the night, as that was where I felt sure the lions were. As we left camp George ritually came forward in his kindly concerned way and checked whether I had the rifle, food and, as always, to ask whether I had a couple of beers or some whisky to wash the dust from our throats and to help us unwind at sundown.

It was about an hour and a half before sunset when we arrived at the Kaume Hills and the views were stunning. The Kaume area is like a natural amphitheatre and we parked on a ledge at the foot of the hills. The Tana, two kilometres away down in the north, looked like a silver snake, threading through the soft, sunlit bush. We decided to climb up one of the rises and to call through the loud hailer for the lions. As we reached the last ledge on the hill's summit, I sensed the lions were near, and spun around, scanning the twin hill which was divided from us by a cleft some one hundred metres wide.

There they stood, all eight lions, standing dramatically gold in the late afternoon sunlight. I pointed, and Mohammed and Sue followed the direction of my hand and saw the pride for themselves. The cubs, unsure of the situation, trotted away into the scrubby cover on the hill, followed shortly by the adults, which left only Growe to stare for some extra seconds before she too moved away.

These lions are wild in the sense that they were wild-born and live natural lives, but their beings are inextricably blended with George's spirit. They may disappear for weeks on end, then arrive, full-bellied, outside the camp – not seeking food, but needing George's presence as, in turn, he dearly needs theirs.

I called to them, but, as wild lions do in daylight, they sought refuge in the thick bush and I knew they would only lose this caution by night. We climbed down and headed up the hill, keeping to its far side so that we did not disturb them, yet also hoping that they would approach us in their own time. Mohammed carried up the meat box in the hope that such an encounter would take place. As we reached the hilltop, I turned on the radio at the planned time and began calling to Rod to report our findings. We could clearly see Kora Rock in the distance, some twelve kilometres away, and the hills dominated the scene below us. The radio crackled in reply, 'Copy you Gareth, what news of the lions? Over.' I stated that they were with us and hoped that they would appear that night. Rod replied saying that he would call back as the crew wanted to discuss whether they would come out that evening to film George with the lions.

He replied a few minutes later that they had decided to try for daytime footage, and we planned the time for calling at first light. I was half disappointed and half relieved at their decision. If they came out that evening they could perhaps shoot the essential footage, but also the morning light would be more visually impressive. I was pleased that we had the lions and felt relaxed that now I had found them we could continue to keep in touch with them as long as it was necessary.

This was our last contact of the day with camp, alone in the heart of hundreds of square miles of bush country. But, as we returned to the vehicle, we did not feel any sense of alienation but one of belonging in the wilds, a sense of self-sufficiency.

That night we made a fire near the vehicle and relaxed with a drink and, later, a hot meal. Mohammed is the most marvellous companion in the bush, and soon the story-swapping began as we sat together next to the fire with the stars lighting up the sky. We sat like this for two hours, calling occasionally to the lions, who were somewhere above us on the rocks.

I stood up to check the surroundings with the spotlight. Sue was next to the vehicle putting away some cans when a sudden bellow of warning erupted from the undergrowth. The lions had arrived – and they were just feet away. Mohammed took over the light as I grabbed chunks of meat and walked on to an open space of rock to throw the meat, calling the lions' names. Gradually they came forward, seizing the meat, impatiently at first but, as their bellies filled, they became more at ease. An hour later all the meat had been consumed and the lions settled back amongst the rock and vegetation, calling softly to each other in the darkness.

These were the sounds that, on top of the Land Rover, we fell asleep to. I felt no fear, only the contentment of resting with the lions around me. I awoke occasionally in the night and could see the shapes of lions moving, or merely resting, looking at the vehicle.

The three of us finally woke an hour before dawn, and they had gone, their departed spirits leaving a hollowness and I realized that we would have to set off quickly to find them again if the film crew were to be able to record the events.

I made contact once again with camp on the radio and told Rod that they should head out to Kaume while I looked for the lions and we would meet to plan how they would film George with the pride. The morning started well. Mohammed and I successfully located fresh tracks within the hour. The lions had followed their route of the day before. They had drunk at the Tana before heading back towards the hills. Their tracks circled behind Kaume and led on to another clump of rocks. We were sure they were resting up among the boulders but had to venture up towards the *inselbergs* to be completely certain.

I walked ahead of Sue and Mohammed and again could sense that the lions were near. I spotted a huge slab of rock and was about to climb on to it to step over a narrow gap when intuition told me to walk around the rock. As I did so, Denis, the young male, suddenly flashed past me, just feet away, followed by his sister, then the surroundings erupted with tawny forms. The lions were reacting as wild lions do and the adult female, One Eye, charged forward to protest the intrusion. To ward her off I shouted at her and slowly we backed out of the rocks and returned to the vehicle. If I had walked over the narrow gap I would literally have stepped over a member of the resting pride.

Unfortunately, by the time the crew arrived, it was again furnace hot and we decided to attempt the filming the following day. I sensed that George was bowing to the wishes of the film crew and was saddened at having to leave his lions behind without any contact and to return to camp to be interviewed.

That night, the lions once again returned to us at the Kaume Hills. I felt that the lions and I were drawn together and that their return was not dictated by hunger, but by slowly developing acceptance. They did not approach us silently, but announced their arrival by calling softly as they drifted down the rocky hill in the moonlight. A sense of calm prevailed as the lions came towards the slab of rock where I stood.

I threw the meat for them and they did not contest for the flesh. It was as though, deliberately, in turn, each lion was calmly taking meat from me. Being there intimately with the lions reminded me of an encounter George and Doddie had experienced at exactly the same spot about four years before which illustrates how it seems that man and lion can be drawn closely together – a togetherness from which both benefit spiritually.

One day, George told his brother Terence how, despite searching, he could not find Growe and her sister Glowe. Terence offered to use the divining pendulum and later announced that Glowe was dead and that Growe was alone at the Kaume Hills. Late in the afternoon, accompanied by Doddie, George drove out to spend the night at the hills. Once at Kaume and as they were heaving bedrolls on to the Land Rover roof, George suddenly heard Doddie calling his name urgently. He turned and saw, only four paces away from Doddie, a large lioness crouching in the bush – it was Growe. She had silently approached and had been watching them. George called to her and threw meat which she immediately seized and fed upon. The lioness stayed with them throughout the night, lying close to the vehicle as George and Doddie slept on the Land Rover roof.

At dawn, all three of them watched a herd of elephants passing by and then, almost as if announcing the end of the magical encounter, Growe suddenly rose, stretched and slipped quietly into the bush, vanishing from sight.

We too, that evening, were enjoying a wonderful, private time with the lions. But, wonderful as it was for us, this was not, unfortunately, producing results for the film crew.

The following morning George and the team arrived early and, though I had an indication of where the lions were, I had not actually seen them. It was decided that George would drive with the crew to an open area below the hills to call for the lions. At the same time Mohammed and I would scan the surrounding areas from high upon the rocks.

Again the heat was too great for the lions to stir themselves and sadly, despite George's repeated calling, no lions appeared.

Mohammed and I then walked back to my vehicle through the bush, some three kilometres away and, quite suddenly, came across fresh tracks. We followed the tracks cautiously through a cleft in the rocks and Mohammed suddenly whistled. I turned to face two of the cubs watching us closely and calmly. The heads of the other lions could just be seen peering through the bush and rocks. They were calm, perhaps lulled by the sun, but perhaps also by the acceptance which I felt was developing between us. As they seemed unusually relaxed in the daytime, we crept out of the rock thicket and returned to the vehicle to call the film crew on the radio. I drove to where George was and led the convoy of other vehicles to where the lions were lying up.

George was quickly wired with a microphone and he called to the lions as we walked into the thicket in search of them. Unfortunately they wouldn't come out – heat again robbing us of the footage so essential for the film. We emerged from the bush with Mike's camera rolling and I'm sure our expression showed how disappointed we were.

The frustration was beginning to take its toll. George, though, was remarkable. Despite the intense heat, the lions' elusiveness, and the pressure of providing what the crew wanted, he seemed amazingly tireless for a man of his great age. Again, I was moved to see how much effort he was putting into making this project a success.

We all returned to camp for a rest. It was decided that once more I should return to the lions – this time with a whole camel carcass which, hopefully, would keep them in one place for a day or two. It was a frustrating period of the project as, apart from Sue, myself and Mohammed, no one else had seen, or even heard the lions.

So, the others were not being spurred on as we were. They had not had the visual stimulus of actually being amongst the lions. I felt that George and the film team should accompany me that evening, as I was sure that the lions would appear at sundown, and that filming would be possible. For one reason or another though, it was decided instead that they would try again the next day. As Sue and I were preparing to set off, Mike asked me again what I thought the chances were that the lions would appear and asked whether he could come along. I told him that I felt they would come and it would be great to have him accompany Sue and me, especially as a most excellent filming opportunity could occur.

That evening, Mike, Sue and I returned to where I had seen the lions in the morning and we certainly appreciated Mike's added strength as we pulled the particularly heavy camel carcass from the trailer. While he and Sue prepared equipment for the night I wandered off into the bush to see whether there was any sign of the lions. I spied, perhaps a kilometre away, a row of heads high upon a rockshelf!

I hurriedly returned to the vehicle to fetch binoculars to confirm that it was indeed the lions and, upon seeing that it was the pride, I cupped my hands and hollered to them in George's way and tone, 'Come on Growe. Look. Come on.' To my astonishment, all eight lions stood up, peered at me, then began to edge their way down the rock towards me. The casual, easy stride of lions is deceptive, and I knew that only too soon they would be with us. I jogged back to the vehicle and instructed Sue and Mike to get organized quickly as I felt that, within twenty minutes or so, the lions would arrive. Mike hurried to prepare the camera and sound equipment.

Just in time we were all settled on top of the faithful Land Rover and I spied Growe about four metres away looking expectantly through the bushes and the gloom of twilight.

Mike glanced at his watch, and looked somewhat surprised. The lions had arrived at exactly the time I had predicted – to the minute.

Soon all eight lions had, in a pincer movement, surrounded the vehicle but still they had not seen the waiting carcass. Eager to get the feeding sequence started and, because of the love of being amongst the lions, I stepped off the vehicle, walked up to the carcass and shook the chain attached to it. All eight lions turned their heads towards me and, as I walked back to the vehicle, they, in turn, walked up to the carcass. That evening with Mike we certainly had a formidable time filming the lions as they fed hungrily and competitively upon the camel. Much later, when little of the carcass remained, the lions began to snarl and swipe at each other in the way they do when only a little meat and bone is left of a kill.

Mike had a wonderful opportunity of filming the feeding pride of lions and made the most of the scene. With him on the bonnet we were able to drive to within five metres of the lions, and achieved the night filming by using a combination of headlights and spotlights.

After several hours the lions eventually sprawled in the bush with only the occasional youngster venturing forward to feed. It was a most memorable evening and left us feeling at one with our surroundings. Later we all slept, Mike squeezing himself, with the camera equipment, into the cab while Sue and I collapsed exhausted on the roof once again.

That night, though we didn't realize it until I saw the tracks the next morning, an old bull elephant had walked silently between us and the sleeping lions. He left only his great rounded tracks in the dust as a testament of his unobtrusive approach and disappearance.

By daybreak the lions had characteristically moved off and I left Sue and Mike filming the sunrise and took off, on foot, following the tracks, having left instructions with Mike to meet me on the road to the Tana River. I walked, enjoying the freedom of being in the wilderness in search of lions.

I followed the lions' tracks for an hour or so before I heard the Nightingale approaching, then I left the lion spoor and trotted through the bush to the road. I climbed into the car and we headed back to camp. The three of us were elated at what we had shared the night before, and were eager to report our experience to the rest of the team.

That evening we were to try once more to film George and the lions at Kaume Hills, a final attempt before he was to be flown to his old haunts of Lake Turkana and Meru National Park to shoot footage of his memories of those regions.

About two hours before sunset the crew gathered at the ledge on Kaume Hills where I had spent the previous nights with the lions. I had not pinpointed where the lions were exactly but within myself I knew that they would appear that evening. Preparations were made for the filming which everybody again hoped would take place during the daylight, but again it was not to be.

George sat on the edge of the back of his Land Rover and I sat nearby ready to hand out meat if the lions arrived. The assistant cameraman, John, sat on top of the vehicle to operate lights if the lions appeared only at night. Soon, with camera, sound equipment and everything else positioned exactly, George lifted the loud hailer and began to call his lions. His voice echoed through the hills and all eyes were upon the rocks, searching for a flash of tawny body or the raising of a head – but nothing appeared.

Gradually, the sun lowered, as did everyone's anticipation and hopes. George continued calling – the only reply being the human voices of those present, which became more audible as time passed and an air of defeat took over. Everybody was convinced that once again the lions would not cooperate. Drinks were prepared and soon most of the people present sat casually on the rock chatting. Later there was talk of leaving, but I was watchful, for I knew that the lions were nearby.

At about eight o'clock, the film crew, Sandy and George,

were debating whether it would be worth staying any longer. I was annoyed at their reluctance to stay, but it was understandable. They hadn't spent nights out in fruitless searches for lions as I had with Lucifer, and they hadn't seen the pride as I had. Mike, however, remained with his camera, perhaps remembering the dramatic night before.

Suddenly, on an impulse, I stood up and walked away from the vehicle, heading straight through the darkness towards a rocky outcrop. I shone my torch, and directly in its beam was the face of Growe. This sense of magnetism is uncanny. Seemingly my subconscious had made me rise and walk within a few metres of an unseen lioness. I called gently to her and then to the crew, 'They're here. They have been for a while.' The lions' reluctance to come forward was understandable. They had sensed that there were strangers present who were excited, uneasy, hoping for the best to happen and in an unusual situation – there was that sense of the unknown.

The lions sensed this apprehension and uneasiness – this mood of excitement. I believe there is a marginal line in the lions' sense of others' fear. It is often interpreted by them as aggression and, for this reason, they had remained in the thickets close by, not calling, just watching from the secret cover of darkness.

At my call, George rose, the crew rushed back to their positions and Sue and Doddie climbed back into the vehicles. Lights were switched on and Mike positioned himself to film as George called to the lions. But still they did not come forward.

Then George's compassion and love for his lions took over. Disregarding the scene the film required, he walked past Mike, and I followed George into the darkness. He threw the heavy head of a camel into the rocks, but still the lions would not come. We moved forward yet again, now almost totally invisible to the others at the vehicles. Despite the growling and snarling row erupting from the cover,

George bent down to seize the camel's head once more and, with all his strength, threw the head again into the air. Suddenly, the silver flash of a lioness crashed out of the undergrowth as she flung herself towards us before stopping, seizing the meat and disappearing with a series of hoarse growls, back to the rocks.

George and I moved back to the others who still stood in the faint circle of light, for we knew that the lions would not, with so many people and 'mixed feelings' present, come forward. The film team were somewhat aghast at what they had just seen and heard, and were more than a little alarmed when George and I had disappeared into the darkness.

It had been a climactic ending to the evening for George and myself, but for the crew there seemed still to be a sense of anti-climax. Again we had not secured the essential footage. The next day, George was to fly with the film crew to his old stamping grounds of Lake Rudolf, now renamed Lake Turkana, and then to Meru. I would, therefore, have some time to monitor the lions and attempt to lure them back to camp where filming would be accomplished more easily.

The following morning at camp, arrangements were being made for the flight to Lake Turkana. Sandy and the film crew were to fly off with George and Doddie and they were to spend a night or so at a lodge on the shores of the lake. George was clearly looking forward to the trip and, for the first time since I had been at Kora, I saw him wearing a smart bush jacket and new leather peaked cap. I could not suppress my feelings of fondness and admiration for him as he confidently climbed into the aircraft to be flown for some hours to the lake and back to the memories which, for forty-four years, had remained in that harsh country.

# 6

◄ ♦ ►

# Footsteps Into the Past

As I waved the crew farewell, I thought of George's adventurous days in that region and the years of exploration of the lake a century before. Lake Turkana, with Mount Kenya and Mount Kilimanjaro, caught the imagination of the nineteenth-century travellers. The German missionaries, Krapf and Rebmann, returned to Europe with fantastic stories of mountains upon the equator, capped with ice and snow, but such stories were dismissed by the prestigious Royal Geographical Society which, however, welcomed with respect Count Teleki's descriptions of crossing blistering deserts to finally reach a great inland sea some one hundred and eighty miles long and twenty-two miles wide.

When George set off with his friend, Nevil Baxendale, in 1934, in the hope of finding gold in the region of Lake

Turkana, they were accompanied by a loyal cook called Yusuf. Yusuf must have been a culinary genius, for, with few provisions, he kept the men fed with products of the wilds such as game birds, wild spinach and mushrooms.

For two months they followed a tributary riverbed, prospecting along the way and, at times, had to resort to eating the berries of *Cordia gharaf* to ward off scurvy.

They found no real signs of gold, but had a marvellous series of adventures. They trekked one hundred and fifty miles around the southern shores of Mount Kulal. Their donkeys were repeatedly scattered by hyenas, lions, rhinos, elephants and thunderstorms. The trek was tough but, in the relentless, tireless fashion of the explorers who had preceded them, they continued in their travels.

On one occasion the entire group of donkeys disappeared overnight, but Tobosh, a Turkana who had joined them and who wore not a stitch of clothing, set off in pursuit. He found the donkeys, just in time. A pride of lions had begun subtly stalking them. Unarmed, Tobosh herded the donkeys together and drove them back to camp. The lions followed and were finally only deterred from their stalking when George and Nevil made their presence known.

Lake Turkana lies at the base of a volcanic system. It is a land of intense heat and wicked winds which blow at some sixty miles an hour. When the wind drops, the heat beats down in waves. The two men had to build screens in the evenings to protect themselves from the swirling sands, and subsequently encountered screens erected by the explorers Teleki and Lieutenant von Hohnel who had been there before them!

The journey became more arduous. A donkey collapsed and died. Supplies ran low and, after two days without food, George resorted to shooting two cormorants. Despite their hunger, our intrepid pair found the taste far too rank. It was, however, relished by the accompanying Yusuf.

Lake Turkana is an extraordinary inland sea which

changes colour according to the wind and sky. In some conditions it appears green and is known as the Jade Sea.

They found no other tribesmen in the area and this was extremely unusual. Eventually, they were visited by some fishermen of the El Molo tribe, which numbered barely one hundred individuals, at the foothills of Mount Kulal. The natives were totally naked except for their young chief who wore, with pride, a red fez, striped pyjamas and had red hair on his arms and chest.

They also found in this region an abundance of game such as the magnificent lesser kudu, but there was no sign of gold and so they pushed on to the lake shore. It is this part of their adventure that George recalled with laughter. Nevil suggested that, instead of walking the one hundred and fifty miles return trip, they go straight across the lake. At first George thought either heatstroke or exhaustion had affected Nevil's senses. That was until Nevil elaborated on his plan. They would build a boat and sail to the opposite shore.

The boat's frame was constructed from acacia branches, and George sewed their groundsheets together for the hull and tailored sails from their bedding. With the donkey boxes as a rudder, a leeboard and oars were constructed and, to the surprise of both of them, their craft floated.

George and Nevil then instructed Tobosh, with his companions, to take all their possessions, apart from a rifle and cooking pot (which was to be used as a bailer) and set off to the agreed landing point. He was also told to slaughter a donkey if they had no other food. Tobosh departed and, that night, Nevil, George and Yusuf slept in a nearby riverbed. In the morning they discovered that disaster, in the form of jackals, had struck. The skin thongs holding their craft together had been chewed through and, in desperation, George had to use acacia bark to repair the boat!

Ten days after the donkeys had set off and after wind conditions became more suitable, they pushed off, rowing until their hands were raw, with Yusuf bailing with the old cooking pot. Much later in the night they heard the croaking of frogs, and knew that the shore must be nearby. Eventually they landed and the following day polished off a half bottle of brandy George's mother had given him for just such an occasion. They then sailed along the shore to the mouth of the Kerio, where they had agreed to meet Tobosh.

Twenty-four hours later, Tobosh duly arrived with all the donkeys intact and uneaten, completing, without mishap, a journey of harsh conditions, considerable distance and relentless heat.

George's admiration for the fierce Turkanas grew immensely during the experience of this expedition and, in gratitude to the men, he left the donkeys as a bonus to the agreed payment.

After a three-day march, George and Nevil found themselves at the District Commissioner's office at Lodwar. The Commissioner was surprised to see the two men. George and Nevil were informed why they had found the shores empty of natives apart from the El Molo. Raiders from Ethiopia had swept across the border in a series of attacks, massacred the men, and taken off back to Ethiopia with women and camels! The District Commissioner was alarmed when George told him of their boating expedition for, only a few months before, Vivian Fuchs had led a geological expedition into the region and left two scientists on South Island. The two men were never seen again. Only the remains of their boat and some clothing were found.

It is perhaps interesting to add that it was on these self-same shores of the Jade Sea where George and Nevil Baxendale had sought gold, that, forty years later, Dr Richard Leakey discovered settlements of *Homo erectus*, the forerunner to *Homo sapiens*.

After a night's rest at Lodwar and after stocking up with provisions, they began the long, sixteen-day journey back to the Marich Pass, the starting point of their travels. At one point, a donkey slipped on a rock ledge, two legs sliding off into a precipice. George leapt forward to seize the beast's ears and Nevil's great strength pulled the flailing donkey back to solid ground.

Four months after beginning their journey, they reached their truck at the Pass.

George and the film crew returned to Kora after a successful trip to Lake Turkana. George had recounted these adventures to the cameras, and had immensely enjoyed the journey into the land of old memories. As he climbed out of the plane, his face lit up when I told him the most recent news of the lions. The day before his return I had found the pride's tracks heading down the Tana River and, having called for them frequently, was delighted when, early the next morning, the lions appeared at camp. In the darkness of the early hours, Mohammed and I fed the lions and their return created an atmosphere of relief and pleasure to all at camp. Perhaps now they would remain close, and I hoped that on George's return he could be filmed, at last, amongst his beloved animals.

Soon after his return, the Director of Kenyan Wildlife, Dr Perez Olindo, flew into camp to be interviewed by Sandy Gall for the film. It was an emotive moment, and an historic one for Kora and George's work when Dr Olindo, standing in the baked bush beside the carcasses of the two slaughtered elephants spoke to the camera of how ' ... in this harsh land, George Adamson has made his home. George Adamson represents the true spirit of conservation in Kenya.... ' and added that before the end of the year it was his wish that Kora would be proclaimed a National Park.

This was unexpected news, and was clearly a wonderful moment for George as this had been his wish for many years. Perhaps now, with this news, Kora would at last receive the full-time protection it really needed and deserved. This positive news was further enhanced when, that evening, with all the camp in high spirits, the lions arrived and we got the first footage of George amongst his lions.

The next planned feature to be covered in the film project was to fly George to the neighbouring Meru National Park where he would lead the crew to Elsa's grave and talk about the *Born Free* years and those that followed.

Once again, the plane departed from the Kora strip with the film crew to meet George at Meru with their Land Rover. I was left to keep in touch with the lions for future essential filming. The evening of the crew's departure I planned to call Growe's pride with George's loud hailer at intervals through the night. I knew that the lions were not far and felt confident that they would return to the camp.

To ensure that I did not miss the lions if they came very late, I decided that I would spend the night in front of the mess hut instead of inside one of the huts, while young Julie also offered to sleep near George's drinks table which was only a yard away from the camp fence. I felt that, despite being tired from the lack of sleep over the past few days, one of us would be awake if the lions appeared or called during the night. That, at least, was the plan.

I stayed awake for hours, calling the lions at intervals through the loud hailer, but there was no sign of them and I eventually fell into a deep sleep. The following morning I awoke with thoughts of the lions' whereabouts immediately on my mind. I got up and, when Julie awoke, asked her whether she had seen or heard anything. She replied that she had woken up several times during the night but had seen nothing despite shining a torch through the fence.

I then thought that the lions must have moved away from *Kampi ya Simba* and had perhaps headed back towards Kaume Hills. Worried that the lions were far from camp and that George and the film crew were due back the following day, I quickly called Mohammed and drove out in search of lion tracks. We had only driven about 700 metres down towards the Tana River when we spotted the pride's tracks on the road and leading back to camp! We left the vehicle and followed the tracks on foot. I began to feel somewhat foolish when camp came into sight!

The lions had visited camp during the night. The tracks led us to the water drum where they drank and, to my astonishment, I could see that two of the lions had walked right up to the camp fence to where, on the other side, Julie had slept. The lions had, no doubt, sniffed and watched her through the wire, while she was sleeping peacefully, and obviously deeply. When Mohammed and I saw where the lions had stood, we both began to laugh, and I called Julie from outside the camp to tell her what had happened, and what she had missed. We all felt a little embarrassed as we chatted, Mohammed and I outside the camp and Julie talking from the inside, as, firstly, we had not woken when the lions had arrived, despite the fact that they had walked up to the fence, all around the camp and drunk water less than fifteen yards from the fence and, secondly, I had rushed out in search of the lions, and their tracks had led us back to camp!

Later, we found where the lions had left the vicinity of *Kampi ya Simba* and we followed their tracks in the Land Rover down Boys Lugga, a stream bed that winds around the camp and leads to the Tana. I had only driven about three kilometres when, suddenly, I spied the lions resting up in the shade of a large acacia tree.

I stopped the vehicle and felt almost apologetic towards the lions for having missed them the night before. They were again very calm, particularly considering that it was daylight. Mohammed passed me some meat and I stepped out of the vehicle calling to them. I walked about fifteen paces from the Land Rover and stopped, encouraging them with more calls to approach me. It was the large cubs who came forward first, grabbing the meat I threw for them.

After fifteen minutes, and twice walking back to the vehicle for more meat, all the lions had fed on what was really just titbits. Only Growe had not come forward. I called to her as I noticed that, when the other lions had taken meat, she had remained lying down, quietly watching. Growe then got up and, with a calmness of spirit radiating from her, walked forward and took the meat I had thrown just a few feet away. She turned, walked a couple of paces, and then settled down in front of me, feeding contentedly.

Mohammed and I left the lions an hour later, confident that they would not wander far and, in our hearts, knew that the pride would reappear at camp when George returned from Meru.

Over the two days at Meru, George was prompted to talk about how he, Joy and Elsa came to live at Meru and another chapter of George's life was revealed.

At Meru, George spoke of the days when, as Elsa grew, suggestions were made that she should be moved to lead a permanently free life on the banks of the Tana in the Meru County Council Reserve, as the region was known at that time.

The area, some three hundred square miles in size, is one of doum palms, of magnificent acacia and fig trees, of great red ridges of rock, and was ideal game country for the lioness to live in. It was, ironically, near the area where Elsa had been born and where George had had to shoot her mother.

At Meru, Joy began to write *Born Free*, the story of Elsa which was to capture the hearts of millions.

In his own autobiography, reflecting about these days, George wrote, ' ... there is no doubt that shared devotion to Elsa had brought Joy and me as close to each other as we had ever been, just as a child might have done – and Elsa took the place of a child in our family album.'

Joy later travelled to London in search of a publisher for her book. In retrospect, it is hard to believe that many publishers turned the book down, but eventually, Collins Harvill accepted it and shaped it, and, after much editing, a phenomenon was born.

While this was taking place in London, back in the bush country of Meru, Elsa had mated with a wild lion, an occurrence which was to add weight to what Joy was achieving in London. In the months ahead, Joy's book was to receive great publicity and part of the reason for its success was the fact that it was a love story – an all-encompassing tale of the love between two people and the creature which, in most people's minds, epitomizes ferocity and great power – the untameable. Very soon, with the success of *Born Free*, Joy set up the Elsa Wild Animal Appeal, using the lioness as a symbol for conservation and, in years to come, this symbol was to raise millions of pounds for the plight of African wildlife.

*Living Free*, the second story of the trilogy, had a similar impact, but it was at this time that Elsa became infected with tick fever and died, only six years old. Had she been affected with babisia, the tick-borne disease, today, she could have been treated successfully – but this was not to be. She died next to George and perhaps part of the strength of Joy and George's bond together died with her. Joy continued to promote her work tirelessly and George was at the point of retirement from the game department.

With Elsa dead, her cubs became a problem in the bush. They took to killing stock, killing whatever was easiest. Their childhood had not been completed, and they had missed the tuition Elsa would have given them. George captured them and relocated them to neighbouring Tanganyika in the world-famous Serengeti. George retired in September 1961, after twenty-three years with the game department, and discovered he had accumulated some nine hundred days' leave!

He told me, at Kora, how he found it irritating to conform to having only visitor's status within the Serengeti National Park. He had, after all, completed years of service as a senior warden in Kenya, but suddenly found he had few special privileges in the Serengeti plains. He was not allowed to spend many nights out in the reserve in search of Elsa's cubs, nor was he allowed to carry a firearm. The main reason for this stricture was because he came across a male lion which was in the final stages of starvation because of a shattered jaw. George shot the lion, so freeing it from its misery and releasing its tortured soul, but when he reported the incident, he was reprimanded and told he could no longer carry a firearm nor interfere with natural occurrences.

Initially, he still had Elsa's cubs to help fend for so, surreptitiously and with the help of a .22 rifle he had stored in a hollowed out tree for just such emergencies, he managed to provide the occasional meal for the youngsters. His concern for the lions, as always, came before unreasonable orders from park wardens!

Joy was at this time working on *Forever Free*, the story of Elsa's cubs, and she travelled world-wide on lecture tours – to South Africa, India, Singapore, Australia and America. During these exhaustive travels, having to overcome the daunting task of talking publicly about her life, she felt Elsa's spirit with her continually and this, she believed, was her major strength.

It was the time of a new black Government in Kenya, and it was a period of unsettlement for George after leaving the young lions in the Serengeti. He believed there would be little work for him in conservation with this change in government. He was mulling over various projects and plans when he received the offer of working with the lions in the film *Born Free*. It was an offer which was, ultimately, to bring him back to Meru and later to Kora, and most of all give a new lease of life to the cause of lion rehabilitation.

This offer also resulted in the auspicious meeting, on both sides, between George and Virginia McKenna and Bill Travers who were portraying George and Joy in the film.

The film-making business was an unfamiliar world for George. He did not enjoy the bickering and personality problems of the people working on *Born Free* and found that, in the long run, they detracted from the essence of the work and their own accomplishment. George grew close to the lions used in the film, however, and was determined to offer at least some of them free lives when the work was over, instead of a lifetime behind bars.

With the film completed, George was given two lions, Boy and Girl, mascots of the 2nd Battalion of the Scots Guard. Another 'film' lion called Ugas was soon to join them and George, with the help of his friend Ted Goss, moved back to Meru, he with his lions, and Joy with the cheetah named Pippa.

He established his camp under the Mugwongo Hill with Joy's camp some sixteen miles away. Cheetahs and lions do not mix, and this is one reason why they decided to have separate camps. George, back at Meru, found relative peace with the swamp nearby attracting herds of buffalo, eland, waterbuck and giraffe, but most important of all he was back with the animals he loved so much.

While Joy and George were at Meru, Pippa, the cheetah, was flourishing, adapting successfully to the wilds, and she produced three litters of cubs. It was Pippa who was the subject of Joy's next two books, *The Spotted Sphinx*, and *Pippa's Challenge*.

Unfortunately, this sense of harmony and permanence was not to last for George, and it changed after an unfortunate incident.

Johnny Baxendale, George's assistant, the son of his old chum, was driving back to camp with Boy. Along the track, he met Peter Jenkins, the park warden, and they stopped their vehicles to talk. Jenkins's Land Rover was relatively open with half doors and windows and accompanying him was his wife and young son, Mark. Without warning, Boy launched himself from the bonnet and attempted to grab the young child. Johnny seized his rifle and then punched the lion in an attempt to get it away. Jenkins then drove off, half dragging Boy along the road before the lion finally leapt away. Mark sustained scratches on his head, and bad gashes on his arms.

This incident spelt disaster for George. He was, initially, told that his lions must be shot and he himself must leave Meru. Just after the incident Boy became ill. He had encountered a porcupine and was badly injured by the quills. George had no option but to leave the lioness and four young lions which he had, in the interim, been given, and the other male, Ugas, at Meru and fly to Joy's house on Lake Naivasha with Boy. Here, at least, the lion could be observed easily and receive treatment. This period in time, for so many reasons, I feel, was probably one of the most strained for Joy and George, and resulted in Joy's request for a divorce on the grounds of cruelty. But, as George wrote in his autobiography, 'As to my cruelty, this must have existed very largely in Joy's mind: she hated opposition of any kind and, no doubt, there were occasions when she found me exceedingly obdurate.'

The years of 1969 and 1970 had been a time of unhappiness and frustration for Joy and this undoubtedly contributed towards her request for a divorce. After a near fatal car accident she had had lengthy operations on her right hand and, because of the injuries, she could not play her beloved piano or paint, two activities which she loved and found therapeutic. She had also been asked by the authorities to abandon her cheetah project at Meru, and blamed George for the fact that she had to leave. When George was planning to return Boy to the wilds, Joy felt that he should just take the lion to one of the areas offered and leave it there, and his refusal angered her. She was also hurt emotionally at this time because her friend and publisher, Billy Collins, had visited two other authors at Naivasha, Sue Harthoorn and Mirella Ricciardi, but had not been to see her. All of these problems caused George to feel the brunt of her feelings.

Fortunately, things changed once Joy started work on her new book, *Pippa's Challenge*, and generally the relationship between them did not worsen as Joy had to accept the fact (if only to herself) that George would return to the bush with his lions.

She channelled her energy with renewed vigour into her books and projects such as the film proposal for *Living Free* and talk of divorce in turn ceased.

Prospects continued to improve for George when it was recommended that he should try the Kora region as an alternative to Meru to continue his lion rehabilitation work.

During the filming at Meru, George had recounted, with sensitivity, much of this period of his life, but much had changed in that reserve since those days. The film crew, George and Doddie, had stayed at the modern tourist lodge, but the luxury did not distract George from the surroundings he knew so well. One evening they listened to lions calling and he couldn't help but wonder whether they were the progeny of Ugas or Girl. On a drive through the reserve a solitary lioness appeared mysteriously beside a track. She stopped, looked at the vehicle, before calmly disappearing as suddenly as she had materialized.

George led the film crew through the thick bush to where Elsa's grave was. Sadly, the track had become overgrown, tangled with thorn, and the local guides were unsure of the grave's whereabouts. George, however, had not forgotten, and they reached the site. Upon seeing it, George was visibly moved. Here he had buried Joy's ashes and probably remembered her words, ' … sitting there, with Elsa close to me, I felt as though I were on the doorstep of paradise'. This memory-evoking site had not been left untouched by man, however, as, some while before the visit, some Somali had stolen a bronze plaque from beside the grave and, more recently, had disturbed the grave, hoping they would find valuables buried there. Sitting there with the film crew and in that aura, the events surrounding both Elsa's and Joy's deaths must have filled George's mind.

On 3 January 1980, Joy had gone for her ritual evening walk, but she never returned. She was confronted by an ex-employee, a Turkana man, who stabbed her to death with a *simi* (a short sword). Her body was found later by her young assistant, Pieter Mawson.

Joy had just completed her book, *Queen of Shaba* which, when published posthumously, told the story of Penny, the leopard, the last of the three great cats of Africa, to which she had successfully given freedom. The account of their life together charmed her legion of readers.

By a strange coincidence, after Joy's murder, Pieter Mawson was also to die a tragic death. He moved to South Africa and then to Botswana. Before I was to embark upon my work and subsequent study of the lions in the same area, Pieter was killed. He died in a vehicle accident in the North East Tuli Block. There is a story told in the area that, after his death, his young widow, Pamela, remembered that Pieter had once said that if he were to die, he would like to become a fish eagle in the afterlife. Pamela left the area but, as she crossed the dry Limpopo River on her journey away, a black and white fish eagle, uncommon in this dry country, suddenly appeared and flew over her. This incident is very poignant and reminds me of the lines of a poem by Francis Nnaggenda. This poem, which Joy had always kept beside her, was printed at the end of *Queen of Shaba*:

> The dead are not under the earth,
> They are in the tree that rustles,
> They are in the woods that groan,
> They are in the water that runs …
> They are not dead.
> When my ancestors talk about the Creator they say;
> He is with us. We sleep with him. We hunt with him.
> We dance with him.

Perhaps this is a fitting epitaph for all who have worked in the wilds, and for the wild, where the dead are never dead but become life. Somehow, somewhere, in the wilderness, the dead never die, but are born again.

After two days at Meru, George and the crew returned to

Kora and once again news of the lions cheered him, especially the story of how Julie and I had slept through the pride's visit to camp. Also in camp that evening was Jerry, the Irish priest from Kyso. He had arrived a few hours earlier with some friends. It was always great to have Jerry in camp, and his presence that evening was particularly special.

That night was a release from the strain of the filming for George and the memories it evoked. And, for me, it was a release from the work with the lions and, in all, a form of unwinding for everyone in camp. Drinks were poured and soon the singing started, with Jerry's guitar accompanying us.

Growe's pride, despite the human noise, were also with us that evening, and some hours before our revelry, George and I ventured out of the camp to feed them. The lions lay within yards of the fence, this time unconcerned by the sounds and people, and again illustrating the perception and uncanny sense these animals possess. In camp that night there was no fear, no trouble or aggression, so in turn, they were relaxed and content.

Jerry finished one song, and as people were asking him to sing another, George suddenly asked him to play 'The Mountains of Mourne', remembering that he and Jerry share the same Irish roots. As Jerry began to play the song, George, in a deeply resonant voice, began to sing. Immediately, in response to him, the lions began to call back to him from the darkness.

At this astonishing response, Jerry faltered for a second in his playing, astounded by what was happening. He continued as George sang on, and the lions called, their roars echoing through the Kora Hills.

Before he started singing and, despite the loud voices and high spirits of those in camp, the lions had not made a sound. But when George sang, they recognized him and responded. Again, I must stress, that these were lions of the wild, never handled by man and perhaps they were responding to

George as they would to a pride male. When he calls, the pride calls with him, proclaiming to the silent wanderers in the wilds that this is their land, as they are in turn part of the land – as in spirit George and the lions are one.

In the last days of the film project, the crew, apart from doing personal interviews with George, concentrated on filming George with his lions as much as possible. Despite the earlier problems and doubts, this was accomplished in time. In the evenings, on the arrival of the lions, George would venture out of the camp to be among them. I would follow (holding an electric cattle prodder in case any of the lions came too close!) and, in turn, would be followed into the night by Mike with his camera and Rod with the sound equipment.

Initially, it was difficult to keep an eye on the lions, Mike and Rod and, at the same time, not get in the way of the filming and sound recording. But quickly each of us became more polished in our approach and it was wonderful to see how Mike, in particular, became increasingly confident amongst the lions. Particularly when one remembers that neither he nor Rod had ever, before coming to Kora, had any previous experience with lions and their complex behaviour.

Filming over for the night, it was with satisfaction and pleasure that we returned to camp.

At this point, I feel that I should recount a couple of the amusing 'behind the scenes' episodes which occurred during the filming. Firstly, one night at camp, while we were making preparations to film George amongst his lions, to provide a rather different angle for filming, it was decided that Mike, Rod and John would park their vehicle outside camp near to where the lions would come to be fed. It was planned that, on the lions' appearance, George would step out of the gate to throw meat to them. The film crew would then record this remarkable scene from the lions' point of view.

Rod, John and Mike, accompanied by Mohammed, drove out of camp a while before the lions' expected arrival to set up their equipment inside the vehicle in readiness and to park at a suitable angle. Then, enclosed in the vehicle, they began their long wait. George had, beforehand, been wired up with a small microphone by Rod, which had to reside on his shorts as he, characteristically, wore no shirt.

After some time the lions appeared, but were nervous, slinking away from the lights, too aware of the unusual presence of the vehicle outside camp to come forward towards George. We waited for a prolonged period, hoping, for the film crew's sake, that the lions would overcome their uneasiness. But it was to no avail.

Rod, John, Mike and Mohammed were keeping as quiet as possible inside the confines of the Land Rover and were all very patient, despite the lack of success. As time went on, it was suggested that perhaps the film crew might need some refreshments and that we ought to discuss with them whether the wait should continue or not.

We had no radio communication with those in the vehicle, but Sandy suggested that he have a 'one-way' conversation with the crew to tell them of our plans by speaking through George's microphone which was linked up to the headphones that Rod had on his head inside the vehicle.

I turned away for some reason at this time and, when I looked back at George and Sandy, I was met by a most unusual sight. Sandy was bending over, seemingly holding a conversation with George's crotch. I tried, with difficulty, to suppress my laughter. It was indeed an incongruous scene, especially with George having a lop-sided grin on his face at the same time as attempting to puff at his pipe.

Sandy though did manage to inform the crew, hidden in the vehicle and in the darkness, that we would serve them with refreshments. Sue filled two of George's ancient silver trays with assorted drinks and then a strange procession took place.

With George at the front leading the way, we stepped out

of the gate with Sandy and me bearing the trays. We passed the pride of lions (looking at us somewhat quizzically) and, with some formality, presented the film crew with the drinks through the windows. Later, when the crew had driven back into camp, filming over for the night, the 'crotch conversation' was told to the merriment of the crew who at last had a reprieve from their uncomfortable, long wait, crowded in the vehicle.

Another amusing incident took place when the film crew, Sue, Julie, George and I were, despite the possible presence of crocodiles, enjoying lazing in the shallows of the Tana River after a series of interviews had been completed. The water was only several inches deep in most places. However, because of the murky water and because of the scene of us on our backs, feet outstretched and water covering our chests and legs, the depth, to anyone on the banks, would have been difficult to gauge.

Sandy, for some reason, was the last to enter the water. I saw him walk up to the bank and then, to my horror, saw him prepare to dive into the water – he obviously did not realize how shallow the water was. Before I could shout a warning, he launched himself off the bank in a (fortunately for him) belly-flop. Sandy hit the shallow water, there was a loud splash and spray and, as the water subsided for a split second, I saw Sandy lying horizontally in the water, face down with the water barely covering the tops of his ears. He then knelt up, with river sand on his neck and face, pulled a composed look as though nothing unusual had happened.

The incident though was not missed by all of us and chuckles broke out. If a lurking Somali had been watching the scene he would have been totally convinced that white men are quite mad.

The night before the crew were due to leave, we again had a little celebration. The trials and tribulations of the film-making were at last behind us and it was an evening of true companionship. The work on the story of George and his life had bonded us all and brought us close together – no matter from what different backgrounds we had come, nor what different personalities we were.

On the morning of their departure, I took Sandy and Mike on a final drive into the reserve in a leisurely attempt to capture some of Kora's elusive wildlife on film.

We didn't expect much luck, and we weren't worried if we didn't have much success. But, typical of the bush, if effort has been exerted, reward comes in unexpected ways. First we encountered, while driving down the Tana's banks, a baboon troop spectacularly backlit by the morning sun. Mike filmed the tiny black youngsters and their mothers with the swaggering big males nearby. We later left this enchanting scene and stopped at the junction of the Komunyu lugga and the Tana. We walked across a dry section of the river which led to a flat rock outcrop, naturally shielded by low bush and a grove of trees. Mike set up his camera as Sandy and I took out our binoculars and scanned the surroundings for game and bird life.

Minutes later I spied a buffalo herd forging across a series of short rapids. They were quite unaware of our presence, and soon the camera was rolling.

Then we spotted a herd of zebra coming down to drink, followed ten minutes later by a graceful family of lesser kudu – a spiral-horned male accompanied by two females and a youngster. It was truly as though the spirit of the wilds was rewarding us with these lovely, tranquil sights, and in those few hours I saw more game than in all the time the film crew had been at Kora. The kudu drifted away as three warthogs appeared, walking unconcernedly within twenty metres of where we sat.

With all these scenes and others captured by Mike, we set off in search of crocodiles. We spied several, but these great, green reptiles were either too far away to be filmed, or else dipped and disappeared into the silty water of the Tana.

Later, we found a huge crocodile lying exposed upon a

sand bank. I reversed the Land Rover and silently motioned to Mike to follow me on foot to stalk the beast. Soon we had an excellent view of the animal, mouth agape, and the final footage at Kora was completed.

We returned to camp for lunch, then drove the crew to the airstrip where a plane was waiting. Our farewells were heart-felt, for we had shared together a combination of the bush life, elements of danger, and George's life for nearly three weeks.

# 7

◄ ◆ ►

# Of Those Who Walk
# in Darkness

With the film crew now gone, I returned to the routine of
the previous weeks. By this time the security force's
presence at Kora was obvious. Their trucks trundled for
hours through the most isolated parts of the reserve and
frequently, while in the bush, I would meet up with the
forces on foot patrols. The soldiers were always very friendly
and often we would exchange information. They would tell
me where they had come across lion tracks and I would
direct them to where I had found Somali livestock. Despite
the immensity of their work of searching for Somalis, the
army seemed very conscious of their role in the reserve. On
occasions, people visiting Kora from Nairobi, spoke, I

noticed, with scepticism when the conversation turned to the government's attempts to contain the *shifta*'s damaging influence, and their attempts to drive the livestock herders from the parks. At Kora, though, I genuinely felt that these men protecting us and the reserve were not only well-trained and disciplined, but were acting to the best of their ability for the reserve's future. They also held George and his life-long work in high regard.

Julius, the unit commander, would visit George on a regular basis to report his findings and actions. George appreciated these meetings, always offering the men a cool drink in the mess hut, and this gesture, too, was very much appreciated and a welcome reprieve from the hard life these men were living. Julius would always speak to George with the utmost respect, and listen, in turn, in fascination and it was heartening to hear Julius saying to George one day, 'If it had not been for you staying here, George, there would be nothing – no animals, no lions, nothing. We have come to help you because you have protected this place for the animals and, with this, I want to wish you long life.'

George was momentarily surprised by the man's most sincere words. To me the conversation signified, once again, that despite the fact that George had had violent opposition to his work over many years from 'qualified' conservationists, he was, nevertheless, a symbol to many of the local people, the true and ultimate guardians of these wildernesses. He was also a symbol of conservation to thousands of people throughout the western world. George touched both worlds – an achievement shared with very few other 'conservationists'.

George was a subject of African mystique to the local people, for his way of life embodied many of the attributes they traditionally revered. He was termed as a *mzee* – a respected old man. His unbelievable empathy and relationship with lions, an animal which represents life and death in the African wilderness, and his humble existence in a largely traditional situation, bonded him to the local people, for though he was a white man, his life encompassed the fundamentals of the African way.

This is, in Africa, what I call 'active conservation', and is far more acceptable and understandable to the local people than the work of a scurrying scientist from far lands who comes, looks, but does not see, in the African sense, and then leaves with information gathered; taking with him the findings which might have proved of benefit to the local inhabitants.

Instead, George's project at Kora generated interest from the local people and through his work they gained the beginnings of an insight as to why Kora is important. Unlike 'outsiders' George was part of the land. He cared for it deeply and made his home there. The local people recognized that there was a sense of permanency with George and, I feel, they respected him for his strong convictions. To the local people, George gave and did not just take.

An example of this was the presence at camp of a young student named Mohammed. For several weeks Mohammed stayed with us at *Kampi ya Simba*, gaining knowledge for a project organized by his school's wildlife club. Mohammed, with his questioning mind, would accompany us on trips through the reserve and learnt much from his stay and time with George. George, I discovered, from time to time had had other local Kenyan students staying at camp.

Having neglected the search for Lucifer, I was eager to return to the task. After consulting George, I was once again returned to the boundary of Kora Reserve to seek a lion that walked in darkness and who, despite his human upbringing, had found his just reward of secrecy and intimacy as a 'bush lion' as Mohammed would say (meaning a lion, wild and living uninfluenced or affected by George).

One morning I trundled out towards the rusting drum that marked the boundary of the reserve, and the focal area of

Lucifer's wanderings. As I drove out of camp I was eager to discover whether the army had been successful in driving out the many groups of wandering Somali in this section of Kora. On the first half of the forty-kilometre journey I saw no signs of hoof marks or the tracks of plastic-encased feet of men. This was, though, sadly short-lived, for soon I began to spy cattle tracks here, the plate-like footprints of camels there, and I knew that the Somalis were still very active within the reserve, searching for grazing for their stock and hiding in this largely waterless wilderness of thorn and flaking bark trees.

Upon reaching Lucifer's drum I scanned the sandy ground for signs, then searched further up the road, and then down the crude outline of thorns and ever present rock. I searched that morning for three hours and saw no signs of his passing. I then returned to camp, sadly without fresh news for George.

That evening I drove to the cutline and kept vigil upon a rock *inselberg*. In the distance there was another rock outcrop, and upon its rise was the silhouette of a lion, a mocking shape of a stone lion, that only appeared in certain light at sunset. For many nights to come I would, in the last light, gaze at this phenomenon. The place where I saw through the night was elevated and my calls of 'Lucifer, look, come on Lucifer,' would echo, spread and caress the night like ever-growing ripples across water before settling and becoming lost in the darkness of night, like the lion I sought.

That evening I had brought with me the dried remains of a camel carcass, but during the night at this stony place it only attracted a handful of shy jackals and a nervous hyena who, despite the pangs of hunger, would not advance to feed. By the first glimmer of light and as the once triumphant moon paled to nothing, the carcass remained untouched. Again I had not attracted Lucifer.

At first light I drove the morning ritual down the cutline

to the main road, swinging right into the Kitui Reserve and back again, searching and hoping for the full-blown spread of lion tracks, and the slightest scuff, a fleeting meeting between the cat and the African sand. I returned to the cutline, frustrated, but with a mind full of ideas and plans.

On the Nightingale's bonnet I consulted the map of the reserve. I took note of the hill named Mango, a hill which was almost as elusive as the lion. This great rock outcrop could only be seen from the road at two points and was, for the rest of the time, concealed by the bush. When I found the position of this hill on the map my mind turned to Growe and the pride, who would normally rest up on rock outcrops, perhaps enjoying the breeze and visibility from the elevated *kranz* and I thought that perhaps Lucifer too, as the true Kora lion, had the same trait. Perhaps he too rested up, shielded by the shady shelves of rock. Perhaps it was upon Mango Hill that he sat alone, surveying the changing mosaic of tawny camel and piebald cattle wandering below the land he had made his own.

With this in mind I set off again, this time on foot with rifle slung upon my shoulders, map in hand, and the sandy lugga at my feet. I headed towards an unseen hill and perhaps an unknown lion upon its ledges with the signs of his elusiveness in the tracks, old and new, at the hill's base.

I did not find a lion upon a ledge – I did not even sight the hill from the depths of the tangled lugga. Half-way to my destination I heard the bellow of a camel and I stopped and turned. I saw the beast and others around it; I heard the piping call of Somali children separating female camels from their young. Without realizing it, I had inadvertently, in the thick bush, walked into the resting place of the semi-nomadic Somalis. I had found, though not seeking, the people wanted by the army. I continued to stand motionless, not knowing if I had been seen or heard or who or what might be peering (or pointing) at me. Slowly, I turned, searching for a shiny face peeping behind the fortress of thorn, but could see none.

I continued to listen and to look a little longer before slowly backing away, aware of the slightest noise of my feet upon the ground. Because of the uncertainty of the situation, part of me wanted to announce my presence, while the other wanted to remain unobtrusive and undiscovered.

Gradually, unseen by the Somalis, I moved out and back down the lugga. Partly because of the scene I had left behind my mind was filled with tangled thoughts about Kora, its future and my own.

The Somalis were a great detriment to the area. Their stock were ravaging the habitat and the *shifta*'s guns were wiping out the Kora elephant herds and were posing danger for those who lived within the reserve.

I knew that only if the livestock and the *shifta* were removed would beneficial and much-needed conservation work become a reality at Kora.

Eventually, I reached the Nightingale, a welcome sight, standing like the security of one's own home in the shade of the tree. I then drove back to camp wondering if ever the damaging effects of these secretive Somalis and their stock would be overcome. I remembered too the army commander's warning that potentially there is little difference between a herder and a poacher – the difference being merely the hiding of an automatic weapon while herding, and reclaiming it from its hiding place when the potential prize of ivory is within reach.

The Somalis though were not the only 'people' problem at Kora that was on my mind. The assortment of camp visitors continued to arrive unexpectedly at *Kampi ya Simba*. At this point of my time at Kora I wondered why it was that George and his camp attracted a continual flow of somewhat similar visitors, yet from such a variety of backgrounds.

I wrote the following poem some time after I left Kora and I feel it encapsulates the camp visitors' scenario:

They came to see you (for themselves)
They came to meet you (for themselves)
Lion man of Africa.
Some came spurred by curiosity.
Some came for the fear of themselves and
Their real lives.

People, people from afar
Came to seek you
Lion man of Africa.
To some you were a friend
To some they thought they were your friend ...
Some brought pain, others joy.
Some brought laughter,
Others sadness from their troubled souls.

But to all you gave,
To the happy ones you brought further joy.
To the pained you brought relief,
Temporary abatement until they returned
To where they had come.

To some you were a father
Others, another artefact of old Africa.
To friends you were a friend in the truest way.
Some thought you a crank,
Others a saint.
You were their prophet and
To the mocking, the victim of cruel words.

You were a man, a lion man.
You are sensitive, strong, kind
And brave.
But ask little for yourself.
(Perhaps that is why many came and came again.)

Many came but did not see
Others saw but did not understand.
People came to see what they wanted to see
While few would ponder to patiently
Understand your deeper self.

The old and the young they came.
The poor and the rich they came.
How did you attract so many?
You attracted all.
But was it the beast or the man they sought?

In the stillness of the night,
If their eyes and minds were opened
They would have found both
The man and the beast.
The man of the lions.
The lion man of Africa would be
reflecting in the eyes of those
who came to see you (for themselves).

More to themselves than anyone else, some of the visitors would justify their stay at Kora by stating that they were helping George with camp chores and, in turn, I realized that they were preventing the local staff from becoming more responsible for the running of the camp. For example, to my knowledge, very few, if any, of the staff knew how to use the radio telephone in emergencies.

Instead of being a Mecca for wildlife enthusiasts and conservationists, a place where the exchange of ideas and experiences takes place, *Kampi ya Simba*, in the time that I was there, was often 'used' by people and, having such people in camp ensured that conflict would arise.

For some of the visitors, being with George gave them a false sense of importance, and possessiveness by young female visitors over the old man was, on many occasions, quite embarrassing. Sadly, I knew that some of the visitors became a strain for George, especially when the camp became overcrowded but, with his typical kindness, he would never say a firm 'no' to a visitor, nor would he turn away any of the uninvited visitors from his camp.

I knew that I could not live long term with such a situation as I had no authority in camp and I was thinking of returning to southern Africa to re-embark upon my own lion study in Botswana.

I did not know what George wanted long term from me, despite the fact that, during the filming, Adrian House had asked me what I had planned for the future and Sandy Gall inquired whether I would consider staying permanently at Kora. I sensed that there were undercurrents that I should stay on working for George and this left me with mixed emotions.

I returned to the rocky outcrop the following night, this time accompanied by Mohammed and young Julie who was still in camp and had adapted to life in the wilds very well over the past weeks. Sue had returned home to England and Julie had asked me one morning whether she could help with the search for Lucifer and, after some thought, I agreed to her offer. Though she had little bush knowledge, her enthusiasm was her strength and her help would, in fact, be invaluable to me. The routine of tracking during the day, returning to camp and then spending the night looking for lions is a demanding one and, quite frankly, much effort is involved in maintaining sufficient water and food supplies, plus the preparation of flasks, torches, bedding, not to mention the more tiring work of sharing watches throughout the night and driving during the day. I did not, though, imagine that Julie would endure the searches for too long, but appreciated her offer for the days ahead.

We scattered small chunks of meat on the rocky slab where I had spent the previous night and secured some camel remains to a tree after dragging it to Sleeping Rock for some ten kilometres.

As the evening began, the jackals became bolder, and as Julie, Mohammed and I sat upon the rock they ventured forward to feed, occasionally crunching smaller bones, all sounds that would attract a lion. Later, Julie moved up to sleep on the Land Rover roof until her turn at watch was due.

Mohammed and I remained and sat talking quietly, as the moon rose. We were both now very relaxed in each other's company and were like old friends together, he stealing a beer under the eyes of his Islamic faith, and I nursing a cup of whisky and water – both these indulgences dissipating the jolts of the road and the frustration of the Lucifer-less days.

During the night, for some inexplicable reason, Mohammed and I would wake up at the same time, he stirring on his mattress inside the vehicle and I on the shared space on the Land Rover roof. Both he and I would call from the loud hailer in the hope that the lion was near and, hearing our calls, would come. The lion was neither near, nor hearing.

Largely because of our tiredness, I suppose, the following day began without great anticipation. The inky night turned to day with no great element of drama. We packed the vehicle and again drove down the cutline, turning right down the main road, searching, then back again. No sign, no sound, no spoor.

That morning I decided that we should try north, back along the cutline and towards the distant Tana River. I felt it was possible that Lucifer was somewhere up the cutline, an area I had not explored before. We had bumped along for some eight kilometres when Mohammed tapped my arm and, staring ahead, said, 'Somalis....'

I looked forward to catch a fleeting glimpse of four shapes seemingly diving into the tawny thorn country. Then, a herd of camels came into view. I suggested to Mohammed that we talk to the herders and that he should call to them to ask about lion spoor. I told him to shout that we were not *askaris* (soldiers) but a *muzungu* (white man) looking for a lion.

I slowed the vehicle and switched off the engine and Mohammed climbed out in a deliberate manner, on to the now deserted road. He shouted into the quietness of the bush in their language, 'Friend, look I have no rifle. I am not *askari*. I am with a white man, come and talk to us.'

Like ghosts in the daytime, the Somalis first replied, then

slipped on to the road within the blinking of an eye. Mohammed strode casually up to them, while they stood clutching their sticks, their *kangas*\* and their spears. Telling Julie to remain in the vehicle, I too got out and approached the Somalis, watching their uncertainty, but at the same time, trying to appear unconcerned about them.

The group was composed of four young men. They had proud, fine features, wavy, loosely curled hair, but each possessed the eyes of a tormented dog, wanting contact, yet shying away from a kindly hand. I knew that both Mohammed and I should be at ease, as the men's reception and reactions would be fast and over-zealous. Their faces were the faces of the land. They were people who lived by the laws imposed by the wilderness and who survived by obeying the restraints; and by knowing the risks. They too were pursued animals who would leap away with the grace of a gerenuk at the advance of their hunters, the army and the game department.

The Somalis are, historically, defiant people and though they were inflicting such harm on the habitat in Kora with their livestock and with their guns on the elephant herds, one could not but admire their great resilience and capacity for survival.

The four young men were living some twenty-five kilometres from the nearest permanent water, the Tana River. They were subsisting upon the milk of their stock, and precious little else. Home was a bare space of bush encircled by thorn and, because of the army presence, they rarely lit fires. Traditionally, they do not kill wild game for food and are devout Muslims, praying to Allah several times a day.

As I studied the men, Mohammed continued in his questioning and spoke to them about Lucifer. Yes, they knew this lion who leaves a scuff in his tracks but, strangely, this lion had never attempted to kill any of their stock, but

---

\* *Kanga* – cotton sarong of a Somali male.

they often heard him calling in the night. After they had told us this, I beckoned the nomads to come towards the vehicle, but they were still very unsure and indecisive. Eventually though, at the mention of tobacco, they came forward. Seeing Mohammed's wariness of these people I, like him, walked alongside them, rather than in front. Their movements were jerky and it was as if with the slightest provocation their fragile composure would snap and their behaviour would become violent.

I gave them tobacco, promising more if, whenever they heard my vehicle in the days ahead, they would show themselves and give me news of Lucifer. Mohammed told me that the following day they were to trek with their stock to the Tana, avoiding the army along the way, and after watering the stock, would return to the cutline, covering long distances during the night and day, to their bush home of the past three months.

After standing uneasily with us for a while, the four Somalis departed back into the bush and, once again, the surroundings suddenly seemed empty of other human presence – in reality it was just concealing and shielding the people who are shaped by the wilderness.

My day-to-day routine of searching for the lion, coupled with the Somali and army presence, made me think of what could happen while I was out in the bush with Julie and Mohammed. The *shifta* were still inhabiting the Kora Reserve, my movements were largely predictable and undoubtedly were, I feel, watched keenly by unseen eyes.

Whenever out in the bush, I carried one of George's weapons – an old .303 from his game department days. I did so for my own and my companions' safety. I did not make it obvious that I had a rifle as, technically, I did not have authorization to carry one. But I am sure that the army knew and turned a blind eye. The reason for this was because they knew that I was wandering across great tracts of remote bush, out of contact with camp or the army, potentially vulnerable to the other unseen inhabitants of this wilderness.

Often, while standing vigil at nights in the bush, I would think about the easy target I presented to the bandits. If it had not been for the love of lions, the passionate challenge of finding Lucifer to remove a dangerous, tightening radio collar, I would not have undertaken this task.

George, having spent so many years at Kora with the constant presence of the *shifta*, accepted the potential dangers as a fact of life, and this reminds me of an incident he told me of one night as we discussed the *shifta* situation.

Back in 1979, the *shifta* attacked a camp on the far side of the Tana. The camp was burned to the ground, three African staff were wounded, and a fourth African and a young German minding the camp were killed. Because of this incident, the authorities posted rangers to stay near George's camp, but before they could be installed, the *shifta* had already planned to attack *Kampi ya Simba*.

George had, at this time, sent his driver, Moti, to the nearest village of Osako to buy camel meat for the lions. This journey, following the Tana's banks, usually takes two hours. But three days later Moti had not returned. By coincidence Johnny Baxendale, George's assistant from the Meru days, had flown into Kora and, hearing the news, offered to take George up in the plane to search for the missing vehicle. Eventually, having found no sign of the vehicle along the road, they flew over the village, and saw the Land Rover standing next to a cluster of huts. George and Johnny dropped a message to the driver, telling him to meet up at the nearby airstrip.

Here they landed, and Moti explained why he had not returned to camp. As he was about to leave Osako, a friend came forward to warn him that a group of thirteen *shifta* were planning to ambush him, seize the Land Rover, and drive into camp. It is customary that whenever a vehicle is heard at *Kampi ya Simba* the camp gates are automatically opened by the staff, and the *shifta*, knowing this, planned to drive into the camp to kill and ransack.

Once the rangers were camped with George, it seemed less likely that such incidents would take place but, at the same time, *shifta* were raiding villages and, on one occasion, an incident broke out between rangers and *shifta*. In this conflict, one *shifta* was wounded and captured, another killed, and a member of the platoon was brought to George for treatment of a bullet wound in the leg.

These worrying times calmed somewhat when, one day, George's tracker, Abdi, returned from the village with the news that George was no longer on the *shifta* hit list. The Somalis had decided that he should not be killed mainly because he was of financial benefit to them. George spent much money on camels and so created relative wealth amongst the locals. Camels cost some £150, and when the lions visited camp regularly, he would buy one a week.

While I was at Kora, I did feel that the mystique of George and his relationship with the lions also acted as some kind of safeguard against *shifta*. In a sense the lions are George's guardians, as he is in turn theirs.

I too had contact once with the work of the lurking *shifta*. The incident took place two weeks after the army had shot dead two poachers, and it was possible that what I was about to encounter could have been retaliatory action by the bandits who were seeking revenge upon either the game department or the army.

The two poachers had been suddenly confronted by the army on a patrol and, with the 'shoot on sight' policy now decreed, the two men were killed, though it was suspected that another had escaped unharmed. The army commander who had led the patrol told me of the confrontation, and explained that they had not buried the poachers – their bodies had been left in the bush as a macabre warning to other bandits that the army was serious.

For many days, on the way to the cutline of the reserve, I

would pass where the killing had reputedly taken place and see the symbols of death in the bush, the vultures perched upon the trees with full crops.

My encounter took place one evening as, once again, I was driving out to spend a night listening and watching for Lucifer. I was accompanied by Julie and a young Englishman, Neil. I was about half-way to the cutline and was anxious to reach the area as the shadows were lengthening and sunset was half an hour away. We were talking generally about the search for Lucifer when, as I turned a corner, I was suddenly confronted by a barricade of logs in the road behind which, at intervals of fifteen metres, were six more sets of barricades – the work of *shifta*.

Instinct took over as I automatically changed down a gear, and slammed my foot down upon the accelerator, steering the Land Rover towards the weakest point in the barricade.

Once through the first, I sped through the second and continued around the remaining piles of tree trunks and branches, half expecting at any moment to hear the outbreak of rapid fire behind us. I remember turning to the others and seeing the startled face of Neil, while Julie's strong sense of self-preservation had forced her low down on her seat so that she would be out of sight.

After I was through the barricades, I sped away. At the same time I was sure that the vehicle had been damaged and continued until I was well away from the site of the barricades.

Julie, Neil and I broke out into excited talk, a release from the shock of the incident, and later I explained to them why I had driven through the roadblocks. Neil, when first seeing the barricades, had shouted, 'Stop. Turn around, turn around....' This is a natural reaction, and one which the ambusher preys upon. I explained to him why one must do just the opposite.

When the possibility exists of being confronted by the sudden appearance of such attackers, there is one main rule:

'Don't stop – don't even slow down – drive straight through at speed.' In building barricades, the ambusher chooses his spot with attention to detail and wants to create the greatest visual impact, thus forcing the driver to instinctively slam on brakes. At this, the bandits or terrorists, positioned from behind, begin firing at the vehicle and its occupants.

Later, I stopped the vehicle and checked for damage. One shock absorber had been wrenched out of its fitting by the hard wood and two leaves in the front right spring had been snapped by the impact. On seeing this, I told Julie and Neil that we would continue as planned to spend the night at Sleeping Rock, and at first light we would drive to the game department and army camp outside the Kitui Reserve to report the incident.

Fortunately, we reached Sleeping Rock just as the sun touched the horizon and, typical of a Kora evening, the night fell quickly. Later, as I sat on watch, gazing at the stars, and listening to the usual night sounds, I remember thinking that it was incredible that we sat amidst such seemingly peaceful surroundings, when just a few hours before we had passed through a situation of such potential violence.

What I did not realize then was that the incident was to bring me closer to finding Lucifer – with typical African fate.

The following morning we left Sleeping Rock early and, later, we reached the army camp. Unfortunately, the commander and his soldiers had just, minutes before, left on a patrol into the reserve, and so I left a note stating where the barricades were, and at what time we had come across them. Then we set off back into the reserve. It was, at this time, that fate was about to play its part.

Half-way through the Kitui Reserve I spotted, some one hundred metres in the distance, the form of an animal on the side of the track. I slowed down, then drove forward at a walking pace and discovered, to my joy, it was a small lioness, walking towards us. I stopped the vehicle and peered through the binoculars to study her closely. I knew, in my

The mess hut.

With the Adamson lions in Botswana
(*Bruce Petty*).

Furaha, with her brother Batian and her sister Rafiki, revived many
memories for George as the past coupled with the future.

Julie Davidson with Furaha at Tawana camp, Botswana.

One of Growe's pride peering through the lion-fence at *Kampi ya Simba*.

One of the Kora elephants slaughtered by poachers.

Hippo: a victim of drought and overgrazing.

A *Kampi ya Simba* resident — a Marabou stork.

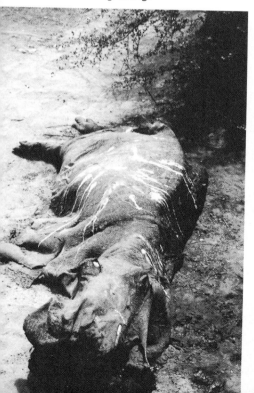

George's cub eating goat-meat at Kora (*Jane Hunter*).

The elusive Lucifer!

Elephant jaw toilet à la Kora.

Playing with one of the trio of cubs.

George and Mohammed take the cubs for an early morning walk.

A young lioness from Growe's pride drinking from the water drum.

With George, on the banks of the Tana river *(Jane Hunter)*.

A passing troupe of Somali nomads and their camels.

George feeding one of Growe's pride.

George Adamson – lion man of Africa.

heart, that she had to be the lioness whose small spoor I had occasionally seen with Lucifer's and indeed the same lioness who had been observed with the male by the game department sergeant at the drum. I drove closer to her and was astounded when the lioness showed so little fear, as she was, we always thought, a wild lioness with no connection to George's lions. This sighting soon made me think differently.

She slipped into the bush and I stopped the vehicle adjacent to where she had left the track. I hauled myself on to the window frame to see whether I could spot her. Julie whispered to me, 'There she is,' and between branches and grass I could just make out the form of a lioness, not twenty yards from where we were. I asked Julie to take out some meat and I began to call Lucifer's name. I felt that there was a chance that he could also be nearby. But there was no response.

I then checked the lioness's spoor in the sand and, undoubtedly, this was Lucifer's female. I flung the meat on to the road and drove forward to check for other tracks, but there were none – she was alone. Nevertheless, I was thrilled to have come across her so unexpectedly, and particularly so to find her unconcerned by our presence.

This encounter dispelled most thoughts and talk of the incident of the night before, and I drove onwards, leaving behind some meat in the hope that the lioness would return to where she had stood and would find the offering.

Only thirty minutes later, I stopped again. I had found a line of lion's spoor upon the road. It was Lucifer's. As I studied the tracks closely, I discovered that he had walked over our tracks from the same morning, which meant that he had been here, perhaps only an hour before. I called once again, hoping he was close, and after waiting some fifteen minutes again left meat behind on the road.

It was incredible that, because of the ambush incident, I had been given the sighting of the lioness and evidence of Lucifer's whereabouts. I was now even more determined to search for the lion, despite the incident of the night before.

As a conclusion to the ambush episode, I later discussed the matter with the army commander and asked, if indeed the *shifta* had even been present, why they had held their fire on us. He replied that it was probably the fact that we were recognized not to be the authorities. Searches took place for the people who had built the barricades, but they have never been found, and have disappeared – like phantoms in the wilderness.

# 8

◄ ♦ ►

# The Decision in the Dark

One evening, accompanied by Doddie, George and I drove out of camp to the Tana River. We had planned to spend a night out in the bush, calling and waiting for Growe and the pride to appear. The search was not one of those intensive 'Lucifer' nights but perhaps an excuse to have a change from the camp and to enjoy an evening of peace and quiet companionship. This time, I believed, marked a point in George's assessment of me as an individual and, on reflection, he must also have summed up my passion for lions and my dedication to the cause of conservation in general. It was on that evening that George was about to divulge his true feelings on my, and Kora's, future.

As previously mentioned, during the filming of George's life both Adrian House and Sandy Gall had asked me about

117

my future plans and, later, whether I would consider staying on, full-time, at Kora. With Tony moving to Tanzania, George needed a man to work with him and, ultimately, after him. My answer was noncommittal. I had seen Kora's situation and while I liked some aspects, I found others unfavourable. There were the bad and the good – for example, the uncontrolled influx of visitors, balanced with possible plans and projects for the area, the unstable security situation of the reserve, balanced with the Director of Wildlife's promise that Kora was to become a National Park. I was basically unsure about the future of Kora and my role there, and deep down, felt it would be wiser to return to Botswana and re-embark upon greater preservation of lions in the North East Tuli Block where so much work still needed to be done. I felt, in my heart, that I did not ultimately belong at Kora and, in retrospect, perhaps this was a feeling which I should have acted upon.

At Kora there was constant reference to why Tony's work in the reserve no longer exists – reference to the 'people problem' and the over-involvement of those unimportant to George's work and the lack of involvement of those crucial to the future of Kora. I was really 'on the outside, looking in', but inadvertently had become more.

It was obviously an honour to be thought to be the ideal heir to George, but what probably made me not dwell on the issue was that I had not heard from George himself what he felt. That was until that evening on the banks of the Tana. Today, despite the words he was about to speak, I wish I had chosen to leave Kora earlier, as I had initially planned, as undoubtedly it would have saved much heartache for both ourselves and those around us.

That evening, when the sun had sunk below the horizon and the stars were lighting the inky night, George, somewhat uncharacteristically, and perhaps prompted by images and memories produced by the filming, spoke about Kora's future and his true wishes. He quite suddenly, and frankly, told me that he was not 'going to live for ever' and expressed his worries about his lions and Kora's future.

'I'm getting rather long in the tooth now, Gareth, and I want you to continue my work if you want to. I don't want my work and Kora to collapse when I die, and I think you are the most suitable man for the job.' I was deeply moved by his words and my thoughts of returning to southern Africa were pushed from my mind.

George was offering me a chance to become an intimate part of his life's work and, with it, his blessing and the honour of continuing his work. At that moment, in a peculiar sense of gratitude, I felt particularly close to George.

He was, like me, an emotional man, despite people's frequent reference to the typical English reserve. That night I witnessed again George's great sensitivity, his reaction to a passage from my book, *Cry for the Lions*. As mentioned earlier, George and I wrote two similar passages with a time difference of some twenty years. That night I reminded George of his words, '.... than to grace some graceless abode ... ', and then read my passage, '... a lion, an animal much older than mankind, is still today killed for pleasure.... ' I read the passage purely to share with him our common feeling for lions. Upon closing the book, I looked at George and saw him turn away. His eyes were moist and, momentarily, he could not speak. Suddenly I realized the closeness of our beliefs, and the fact that his passage and mine had been written, and spoken, by kindred minds and spirits.

Later, on that memorable evening, the three of us drank to each other's health and long after Doddie and George had settled to sleep on the Land Rover roof, I stayed wide awake, the jumbled thoughts racing through my mind. The immensity of the situation was bewildering. I was the outsider, looking in, the newcomer to the country, and initially a stranger to George and Kora, but through him I had gained acceptance. If only fate were to be as kind.

The following morning, elated by the conversation of the

night before, we drove, purely for pleasure, along the Tana's banks. The Kora wildlife was unusually abundant and bold. Herds of waterbuck stood watching, kudu skirted from the bush, and we watched as baboons played out their pantomimes from their stage in the trees. It was, I felt, the beginning of a new chapter for both George and me, and for Kora. Still, a slight sense of unease remained.

It was soon after George had spoken to me about his wishes that I began to divide my time between searching for Lucifer with Julie, and working on plans and proposals which could possibly enhance Kora's future. With George telling me that he wished me to stay with him at Kora, ideas flowed from me, ideas that could be applied in this chunk of Kenyan wilderness. I had also planned a trip to Britain and southern Africa, partly for a rest and to visit a friend, and partly to gather equipment and information relevant to my future work in the reserve at Kora.

One of my initial plans was to instigate a lion census. I had learned, since being in the area, and despite George's long work, that there were remarkably few signs of wild lions in the seven hundred square kilometre reserve. Perhaps the effect of the Somalis and their stock had been so great over the years that a population of lions had never been allowed to reach an optimum size relative to the natural prey available, because of poisoning and destructive snaring. The pressures, at first glance, must be huge as lions are remarkably resilient beasts and populations can bounce back, if the artificial regulating pressures are removed.

At Kora though, after hundreds of hours looking and searching for signs of lion tracks, I knew that the lion population in the area was extremely low, consisting probably of only George's lions and a handful of wild ones. This was my impression, but I wanted to confirm this through a study and the information of the imbalanced lion population (along with the demise of the Kora elephants) would be a further reason for the Wildlife Department to make Kora a protected National Park – the Adamson National Park – that's if I had my way.

I planned to find the true status of the lions in Kora – after all, Kora was synonymous with lions and George Adamson. I intended achieving this census by using sound equipment which had been used in the North East Tuli Block to attract lions when, for example, snares were removed or radio collars fitted on lions for research purposes. The method requires the use of a bait within a specific area where fresh lion tracks have been seen. Feeding sounds of hyenas and jackals are then, in turn, played through loud-speakers, luring, if present, the ever-opportunistic lions to a bait.

My second plan was to initiate the concept of wilderness trails at Kora, a subject which I have previously mentioned. The establishment of such a concept would be beneficial to Kora's future. A form of tourism, in a low-key way, would be developed, and in the government's eyes, the area would have justification for its existence.

The thrust of the trails would be focused upon Kora's special qualities, the wilderness spirit, the remoteness, and the recognition of one's own closeness with nature in this unique place.

I also planned to start a financial 'adoption' programme for the three small cubs. What I was proposing was that an outside benefactor, whether a private individual or a company, could adopt, in the financial sense, the entire costs of feeding, medication, etc., for the cubs until they reached the releasing age and could fend for themselves.

The cost for such a project is, after all, high and I had realized, after some calculation, that it would cost George about twelve thousand US dollars to rear the three cubs to the age of two years.

Lastly, to alleviate the pressure of visitors to George's camp, Doddie and I discussed with him the idea of self-help *bandas* (huts). Visitors, I felt, should be seen as a resource to be utilized. If a separate camp was established for visitors, not only would strain be taken off George, but revenue could be made and employment created.

What was needed, we felt, was a small, fenced camp offering basic accommodation at a reasonable price. A camp attendant would act as overseer, help with cooking and, possibly, guide the visitors around the reserve. Visitors, if paying to be at Kora, would only stay for just a few days, an acceptable period for George, and then they would leave. At the time, visitors were costing George money, as some of the young visitors stayed at camp for long periods and did not contribute towards the camp's expenses.

While I was working out the details of these proposals with George and Doddie and alternating this with tracking down Lucifer, the days ticked away and, almost without realizing it, I was due to fly to the United Kingdom.

I left Kora one morning with Doddie, promising George that I would be back within a month. I would be armed with additional information for the proposals I was preparing for the government and with the lion-luring sound equipment.

I was confident that this would help me find Lucifer. With great fondness I said goodbye to George as he said, 'See you soon, Gareth.' I drove away, leaving behind me the camp staff, a line of waving black figures with George standing in the centre. It was a peculiar farewell as, in my mind, there were reservations about the aspects of the work in the future, and I wondered why such projects, similar to my own ideas, had not been planned in the past. My ideas were, after all, hardly original. Again, there was that lingering feeling of uneasiness.

Another thought that stayed with me on my departure from *Kampi ya Simba* was that along the road to the cutline, I would find evidence, once again, of that unseen lion, Lucifer. But I certainly did not anticipate what was actually to happen.

Just as I was approaching Cheetah Rock, a dramatic *inselberg* about half-way to the cutline, I saw a mass of lion tracks criss-crossing the road. Excited, I leapt out of the car. The tracks were extremely fresh, signs of not only Lucifer but the little female as well. I climbed on to the Land Rover bonnet, and then on to the roof to scan the surroundings. I knew that these lions were nearby. Perhaps now, at the point of my leaving Kora for a month, I would finally see Lucifer – after a search of ten weeks!

With Doddie standing on the ground inspecting the spoor, I felt the lion's eyes on me. I turned and looked up towards the boulders scattered round Cheetah Rock and called for Lucifer. As I did so, a lion stood up from a rock high upon the *inselberg*. I called to Doddie, 'Look, there they are,' and I continued to call, 'Lucifer, look, come on.' The lion was the small female and, instead of moving away, she seemingly obeyed my calls. She rose, stretched, then, completely at ease, deliberately slipped down the hill, almost as if she was about to move down the rock to approach us.

I was amazed by her behaviour but, after some minutes, I lost sight of her, and added to this, there was no sign of Lucifer. With a certain amount of impatience, I walked with Doddie up to the rock. We climbed on to its ledges, expecting at any point to come across the lions. We continued to the highest point we could reach and then stood surveying the area below us. It was like a dream – the lions had vanished. Later we climbed down the rock and inspected the ground at the base for spoor. As I reached the road we had just driven along, I found the spoor of Lucifer and his female crossing the track. There was no sense of haste in their strides, they had just wandered away from the rock with their unaffected natural gait, seemingly unconcerned by our presence.

Again Lucifer had eluded me, almost as if he was deliberately leaving a lure for me to return to Kora. The behaviour of the lioness on the rock again baffled me. She had seen both Doddie and me leave the vehicle and had a clear view of us, but she had behaved calmly, instead of grunting and rushing into the bush as wild lions normally do when confronted by man.

So it was with a mixture of joy and frustration that I left Kora, wondering about that elusive lion and the uncertainty of the future.

# 9

◄ ◆ ►

# A Lion Lost No Longer

After two days in the bustling city of Nairobi, I flew to Britain. After the long months at Kora, I needed, both physically and mentally, a rest from nights of little sleep and time to think about the future. I was drawn to visit Britain, partly to meet up once again with my close friend, Jane Hunter. Jane and I had lived together in the North East Tuli Block where we were both working and, later, we undertook together the long journey described in *Where the Lion Walked*. However, the effect of working and living intensely together on such projects for months on end, under harsh conditions, proved damaging to our relationship. Sadly, we separated, but I inwardly hoped that our period of time apart would be temporary and ultimately beneficial to us. My return to Britain and meeting Jane again proved this to be correct. After two weeks in London, I flew to Botswana happy in the knowledge that Jane had decided to visit George and me at Kora within a month. From Botswana I travelled to South Africa to collect the lion-luring equipment, reports, testimonials and notes and, after a whirlwind few days, I was again flying back to Kenya, hardly rested, but bursting with ideas and hopes.

My first objective, once back in Nairobi, was to have a meeting with the Director of Wildlife, Dr Perez Olindo, at his offices near the Nairobi National Park. Previously, in a letter to Dr Olindo, George had expressed his wish for me to play a role at Kora. We discussed my projects and plans for Kora and I sought his approval for the proposals and, indeed, for my position on the reserve. Within a week or so this was kindly granted, after he had carefully considered the plans and possibilities, and his approval meant that I could apply, with a certain amount of confidence, for a work permit to work full-time in Kenya. With this support, I returned to George and the cubs at *Kampi ya Simba*.

Since I had left a month or so before, Kora had been transformed. Rains had fallen, and from the air the country was like an artist's exuberant wash of emerald green. The rain had revived the dry land, grass was appearing where once only dust had covered the earth, and the trees were bursting with fresh, new leaves, Meeting me at the airstrip was not only Doddie with the vehicle from camp, but the army unit commander, Julius, who gave me news which enhanced the view of Kora I had had from the air. He told me of his excellent work over the past month. All the Somalis and their livestock had been ousted from the reserve, driven with their herds to other lands. He added that his priority now was to seek out any fugitive *shifta* still lurking in secret places within the Park's boundaries. I could not have arrived in this land I had come to love to more optimistic news.

At camp, I found George in excellent spirits and most

happy to see me again. The three cubs had grown dramatically and their greeting was wildly excited. George soon told me how he was taking them for walks out of the camp every morning and around the Kora *inselbergs*, introducing them to the sights, sounds and smells of the bush and, in this, George was undertaking a major stage of their eventual total rehabilitation.

Those first mornings back at Kora, it was a joy to see George gather up his rifle, binoculars, holler for his tracker, Abdi, and then let the cubs out of their enclosure and into the wilds. The three cubs, now no longer babies, but developing lions, were undoubtedly a new lease of life for George and I felt that it was upon these morning walks that I saw George at his happiest.

With the Director verbally approving my plans and my application for a work permit, I was eager to pursue my project of finding Lucifer, using the sound equipment I had brought with me. Unfortunately, however, just as I was about to embark upon this, I had to leave for Nairobi for medical attention. I had developed an extremely painful abscess in the lower intestine, and this kept me away from Kora for ten days or so until it had healed.

Just after my return, I witnessed the arrival of Professor Brahmachary from Calcutta, India. Brahm, as we called him, is one of the most delightful and interesting men I have ever had the privilege of meeting. He is a small man with a flamboyant, lecturer's manner who, when answering questions about his work, marches up and down, emphasizing an important point with a suddenly thrust out hand.

Brahm had visited George once seven years before to undertake a study of the composition and contents of elephant droppings, amongst other things, and now was to spend three months at Kora researching sense perception of big cats and the developing nuances of behaviour in the three cubs. This would complement his comparative study on tiger and leopards in India. It was only his second visit to Kora in seven years because of a restriction placed upon him by financial considerations. I feel it is a shame that funds cannot be made more readily available to a scientist as brilliant as Brahm – scientists who have the ability to unravel the complexities of the natural world and who could produce information to be used, in turn, for the conservation of the wild areas and their inhabitants.

Brahm and I took an instant liking to one another but no doubt presented an incongruous sight to onlookers: picture, for example, our animated discussions on the anal scent glands in big cats, me shirtless, fair and tall, and he, small and clad in heavily protective safari clothing.

Also visiting Kora at this time was the British writer, Robin Page, who shared with me a mutual friendship with the Cheffings in Nairobi. Robin had come to Kora to write about George and the elephant slaughter taking place in Kenya and also proved to be a very friendly and interesting camp visitor.

We had the most entertaining evenings, each of us complementing the other in the style of our storytelling, with Brahm prompting many tales from George, and often correcting and prompting him if he had forgotten a detail, name or place.

On one such evening, Brahm's presence caused George to recount the story of another visiting scientist, Dr Adrian Kortlandt from Amsterdam. Dr Kortlandt's particular interest was the evolution of man and his predecessors, and he had asked George if he could come to Kora to test how early man protected himself from the big cats such as lion, leopard and the sabre-toothed cats. On one particular visit he brought with him a battery-operated propeller to which he would attach branches of whistling thorn, brought in especially from Nairobi. He arrived, amazingly enough safely, at *Kampi ya Simba* in a tiny saloon car.

One day, when George's lions arrived at camp, the

professor placed some camel meat under the blades of the propeller contraption to test his theory. The lions soon noticed the meat and, as a lioness was about to slide a paw forward, the professor activated the propeller. A loud whooshing sound filled the air as the thorn-laden propellers revolved. The lions jumped back and studied this phenomenon for some minutes. As the professor was taking notes and speaking into his recorder about what was happening, the lioness stepped forward and casually flicked the meat away without the professor noticing. George would always add, when telling this story, that subsequently he saw no mention of this incident in Dr Kortlandt's article on the experiment.

Another story, so typical of George, for it combined near-tragedy and comedy, told of the adventure of Hamissi, George's ancient cook, and the Valium pills. Hamissi is a dignified old gentleman with a wry sense of humour, but on this particular occasion he, himself, was the victim.

One morning Hamissi announced to George that he was feeling unwell and had severe headaches and body pains. George gave him two tablets from a bottle marked 'Valium', and left the camp to undertake a search for his lions. When, hours later, George returned to camp, the rest of his staff rushed up to him saying that they thought Hamissi was dying. George, very concerned, inspected his cook and was astonished to find the old man had lapsed into a coma and, indeed, seemed to be passing away. He quickly ordered his driver to take Hamissi to his village so that, if he died, he would be with his family and their love.

Several days after this incident, the doctor, Andrew Meyerhold, arrived in camp and George, during conversation, mentioned the sad, strange case of Hamissi. Andrew asked to see what medication George had given him as treatment, and George produced the Valium bottle. The doctor was shocked to see that the pills were not Valium for human consumption, but a powerful tranquillizer for lions!

Each tablet was capable of tranquillizing four hundred pounds of lion!

Fortunately, after sleeping solidly for some days and causing great concern to his family, Hamissi gradually recovered and, in time, returned to camp, seemingly none the worse for his dramatic ordeal. The tablet bottle was hastily re-marked in bold lettering – 'Valium – for lions only'.

During Robin's visit, conversations also included George's long and mutually benefiting association with Virginia McKenna and Bill Travers, stars of *Born Free*. In 1984, the couple established Zoo Check. The founding of this much-needed organization was largely due to the plight of an elephant named Pole-Pole.

In the late sixties, Bill and Virginia had returned to Kenya to produce the film, *An Elephant Called Slowly*. One of the elephants used in the film was Pole-Pole. She had already been captured as a gift from the Kenyan government to London Zoo, and once filming was over she was sent to take up residence in Regent's Park. After the elephant was taken from Africa and installed in the zoo, Bill went to visit Pole-Pole and, when the elephant recognized him, it immediately became upset. Bill decided not to see her again; she had to form new relationships.

Some fifteen years later, Bill and Virginia were told that Pole-Pole was in a terrible condition. She had been living alone at the zoo for over a year and, in this stressful situation had become very traumatized, often banging her head against the wall of her prison. She had snapped a tusk and lost the other entirely.

Bill and Virginia teamed up with George and Daphne Sheldrick in Kenya in the hope of possibly relocating the elephant from its misery back to its natural home, Africa. When Pole-Pole's plight was reported to the press, donations flooded in.

The zoo did not agree with the scheme and decided to transfer the elephant to the more spacious Whipsnade Zoo.

The transfer never took place. Kept standing in her crate for over twelve hours before the move, Pole-Pole collapsed. She was then dragged out only to hobble round her den for a week, when her leg was examined under anaesthetic. It is understood that she came round from the anaesthetic but as she couldn't get to her feet, the zoo decided she could not be saved.

Her death, and the emotion it evoked, largely prompted the formation of Zoo Check, a trust which today continues to grow, and has done much to publicize and change the terrible conditions under which animals kept in captivity live. Its aims, I feel, merge with George's philosophy – a philosophy which is repulsed by cruelty to animals in any form, believing that all animal life is as precious as human.

Robin stayed with us for a week or so, and his departure coincided with Jane's arrival from Britain. It was wonderful to have her back in Africa again. I collected her from Nairobi airport and we drove back to Kora, receiving a wonderful welcome from the cubs and, of course, from George. I settled to planning my pet project – that of luring Lucifer with the sound equipment. Jane also very quickly settled into the routine of Kora life and, having met George previously when she worked with me on the second book project, I was pleased to see how well they got on, especially when, later in her stay, George suggested that he thought it a most agreeable idea for Jane to join Kora on a permanent basis to help with my work and to undertake her own project.

One morning I was rigging up the loudspeakers and tape recorders, and sorting out the tangle of wires for the sound equipment – to the amusement of the camp staff! The idea of luring a lion by playing sounds was quite bewildering to them and I will never forget the faces of Mohammed and Abdi when I first turned on the tape and the crashing, shrieking noise of hyenas belted out of the cone speakers and echoed off Kora Rock! George was standing nearby and had trouble suppressing his laughter as the staff suddenly stood back in amazement, and the cubs, in their enclosure, scrambled down the resting platform to push themselves against the wire in an attempt to spot the hordes of hyenas and jackals!

With the equipment set up, I took Jane out one evening towards the cutline in search of Lucifer's tracks. It had been raining heavily and much of the road was awash. Nevertheless, quite by chance, we found fresh spoor of three lions, once again at the base of Cheetah Rock. I pulled the loudspeakers on to the top of the vehicle, and scattered rumen contents around the vicinity, as Jane prepared our bedding, the spotlight and some food.

As night fell, I began to play the feeding sounds of the hyenas and jackals and within an hour or so, was surprised to hear the reply of a lion, perhaps three kilometres away in the north. I continued to play the sounds at intervals and, nearly every time, heard the lion calling in reply. An hour later, we heard what I felt was two male lions calling, about two kilometres apart, and I wondered who the other lion was. Delighted by the response to my feeding sounds, I rather impatiently decided to drive down the road. From the sound of the one particular lion's calls, I was sure it was approaching us along the track. I was desperate to see Lucifer for the first time after the weeks of searching and I also dearly wanted Jane to see him.

We set off with Jane driving the Land Rover as I sat upon the cab roof shining the powerful spotlight into the bush. Jane drove for some eight kilometres and I saw no sign of Lucifer. Disappointed, I signalled her to stop, deciding that we would return to Cheetah Rock to see where the lion would appear. I changed places with Jane and drove back. We had driven about three kilometres when I felt the vehicle slide in a particularly wet spot and, because I had not fully concentrated upon the wet conditions, we found ourselves careering into a particularly boggy section of the road verge.

As we stopped, the Land Rover's right-hand wheels sank quickly to the axles and the left side ominously lowered.

I was angry with myself for not having taken more notice of the road. If we could not get the vehicle out of the mire, we would have to spend the night in this position, devoured by mosquitoes and, even worse, would have lost the opportunity of seeing Lucifer that night. All these fears came true – for Jane and I struggled and floundered in the mud and dark for hours. At one o'clock in the morning we stopped our attempts to free the vehicle and fell into a most uncomfortable sleep in the back of the Nightingale, hoping that, at first light, we would be able to shift her.

At dawn we climbed stiffly out of the vehicle, which now was tilting at a most alarming angle, and began the laborious task of digging under the tyres. We gathered piles of sticks, logs and rocks to lodge under the reluctant wheels. But no matter how long we worked in an attempt to free ourselves, the deeper we floundered in the most glue-like mud I had ever had the displeasure of getting a vehicle into. Finally, at midday, we managed to ease the Land Rover backwards, then forwards and, accompanied by the most crude sucking noises, the vehicle lurched very slowly on to harder ground. Both Jane and I were exhausted, but we were elated that we had freed ourselves and, with mud scattering like bullets from the tyres and chassis, were at last on our way back to Cheetah Rock.

It was ironic that when we were just a kilometre from the rock outcrop I saw the spoor of two male lions in the mud along the road. I studied the spoor with a mixture of frustration and acute interest. One of the lions was, quite definitely, Lucifer, and the other, I suspected, was the young male from Growe's pride, Denis.

I then realized that it was possible that the small lioness was in heat, so had attracted the attention of this male but, in doing so, he had confronted Lucifer. As we continued on foot up the road I saw that it was quite obvious that Lucifer was chasing the other male. Their strides were noticeably spread apart, and both lions had kicked up a lot of soil in the chase. I also realized that if I had not got stuck the night before I would have seen not only the two males, but the small female as, further along the road, below Cheetah Rock we found her spoor as well.

We returned to camp just as George was about to send a vehicle out in search of us as we had been away from camp for twenty-one hours. When I drove into camp his body shook with laughter as, covered in dry mud, I described the ordeal of the night before. Intermittently and characteristically he murmured, 'Good God,' as I gave him the blow-by-blow account of the stricken vehicle. He was, however, delighted when I told him of the lions and the very definite results of the sound equipment. He, too, sensed that we were at last very close to finding a most elusive lion and that soon we would be able to assess the situation of the radio collar.

After a brief lunch we prepared for another night in the bush. Despite our tiredness, Jane and I cleared out the Nightingale, filled her with fuel and by late afternoon, with the blessing of George's 'Good luck', we drove back to Cheetah Rock, this time determined not to move for the entire night and to let the lions come to us.

I began playing the calls early in the evening and, almost immediately, there were replies from a male lion deep within the bush some kilometres away. Unfortunately, the elements would again make our night uncomfortable. Jackals moved into the vicinity to investigate the sounds of the tape and the smell from the rotten stomach contents I had scattered, and, as we sat there in the darkness, lightning and thunder approached menacingly from the south. Suddenly, over our resting place on the roof of the Land Rover, the clouds veiled the stars and a torrential storm broke.

Swiftly, we gathered up the loudspeakers and the cassette player and we had just piled all our belongings into the cab when the rain began to fall like bullets. To add to our discomfort, some of the windows in the Land Rover were missing, long ago shaken loose from their mountings by thousands of kilometres of rough tracks.

The rain poured into the vehicle. I grabbed handfuls of plastic bags, a roll of insulating tape, jumped outside and hurriedly covered the glassless gaps. Soon we were both back in the cab and protected from the storm. Later, for just a brief time, the rain lessened and I played the calls once more – this time through the back door of the Land Rover – for several minutes, before the rain began to fall again furiously.

Through the bars of the rain I shone the spotlight around the bush, and saw the reflection of two amber eyes. As I saw them, the storm broke out with increased intensity, forcing me to close the cab door before we became drenched.

Over the noise of the rain on the vehicle I told Jane what I had seen and that I was sure it was the little lioness. Unfortunately, because of the weather conditions I was unable to use the spotlight for the rest of the night. The vehicle rocked and swayed as the storm raged above us, and amidst this, we both fell asleep in the nest of blankets and sleeping bags in the back of the vehicle. We were both exhausted and neither of us stirred until dawn.

The stillness of a new day greeted us. The rain had stopped and, slowly, the dawn chorus of birds gathered strength, their voices announcing the storm's passing. I awoke to these sounds, clambered out of the blankets, pulled open the rear door and stepped out on to the wet ground. There, not ten feet from where I stood, were the pug marks of a lion. As we slept, and with the storm over, the small lioness had walked up to the Land Rover and circled it closely, in inspection, just feet from where we were sleeping.

I hurriedly woke Jane, prepared two cups of much-needed tea, and, with barely suppressed excitement, we drove slowly down the track. We had covered not more than three kilometres when I saw the spoor of two lions freshly imprinted upon the sodden earth.

The lions were here, I could feel them. I drove off the track to an open area, set up the loudspeakers and began playing the calls. We sat on top of the vehicle for fifteen minutes without any response or sign of the lions. I left the vehicle to search on foot, leaving Jane to keep a lookout for the lions from the Land Rover's roof.

I walked away towards a thicket, near the road's verge and there I found more lion spoor. I followed cautiously and was approaching a particularly dense section of bush when, suddenly, an ear-splitting growl erupted from the vegetation just metres to the right of me. Though I was initially startled by the sudden noise and by the closeness of the lions, I recognized the snarl as not one of aggression towards me, but the mating growl of a lion during the climax of copulation. I realized that the lions had not sensed me and were concealed from view by the brush, so I stepped quietly out of the thicket and crept back to the Land Rover. Jane, looking concerned, was standing on the Land Rover attempting to see what was happening. I called to her quietly in assurance and relief and a smile broke over her face. She had heard the startling noise and had, understandably, thought the worst.

I climbed back on to the roof to sit with her and to come to terms with the excitement of finally finding Lucifer. After ten minutes we headed the vehicle back towards the road where I had heard the lions. I was steering around a slight curve in the road and there, at last, was the lion I had been seeking for nearly three months. Lucifer, the lost lion, the lion presumed dead for so long, stood on the road with the small lioness in front of him. My joy and relief in sighting him cannot be described.

Having intently studied photographs of this lion, though never having actually seen him, his appearance was strangely familiar. I recognized his angular head, and then the dark mark around his neck, the legacy of a tightening collar which, I realized with relief, he must somehow have rid from his neck. The absence of this collar made the sighting even more rewarding as he would now not have to be subjected to the darting operation which would have been required to remove the collar.

The lions slowly moved away and again I could clearly see the injuries to his neck. Despite the ugly, discolouring marks, the collar was gone and he was left with dark scars where it had once been. At last we had found him.

The following days and nights were ones of considerable excitement for Jane and me. After the initial sighting of Lucifer, we returned to camp and eagerly told George the news. His pleasure was as great as my own. I asked him to come with us to try and see the lions for himself and, with Brahm piling into the back of the vehicle, we drove out towards Cheetah Rock, pointing out the lions' spoor as we approached the area. We then drove into the clearing where we had last seen the lion, then stopped the vehicle to listen for the sounds of mating to betray the lions' position. Lions copulate frequently and over long periods of time, mating on an average every twenty minutes for as long as twenty-four or forty-eight hours. We waited for about half an hour then, to my pleasure, heard the spitting mating growl from deep within the bush. I encouraged George to call to Lucifer, hoping that the lions would react to his voice and approach us but, sadly, as the minutes passed, there was no reaction. We waited until we heard them mate again then I drove as far as I could into the surrounding bush, but the trees were too dense and we could not venture towards where we knew the lions were lying.

Sadly, we were forced to return to camp but, on the journey back, George suggested that I return the same evening with bait and try to lure the lions to feed so there would be a chance the following morning of a sighting.

Mohammed accompanied Jane and me that evening. He was as excited as George that I had finally located Lucifer

and was eager to see the lion for himself. As we approached
the area where I had last seen the lions I asked Jane to drive
while Mohammed and I climbed on to the Land Rover's roof
to see, as we drove past, whether there was any sign of the
lions. Suddenly, as Jane drove on, I saw, deep in a thicket,
the protruding head of Lucifer. I tapped on the cab's roof for
Jane to stop and I pointed to the lion for Mohammed.
Instantly, he too saw the lion and, gripping me tightly as we
balanced on top of the Land Rover, exclaimed breathlessly,
'Yes. Lucifer – it's Lucifer.' He was overwhelmed that it was
the lion he had helped rear and clapped me affectionately
on the shoulder as I signalled to Jane to drive on a short
distance.

Along the way we had been dragging a goat carcass behind
the Land Rover. Jane turned the vehicle so that we could
chain the carcass on to a low tree. As we did this, scattering
the   strong-smelling   rumen   contents   into   the   bush,
Mohammed began to call the lion. We then drove some
twenty-five metres from the carcass, positioned ourselves so
that, if the lions came to feed during the night, they would
be within full view of the vehicle's headlights. We then
snapped open three beers and relaxed as the sun lowered and
pushed the last of the day's light through the trees, and the
wait through the night began. Within half an hour we heard
the mating snarls and Mohammed, upon hearing this, smiled
– his face beamed with unashamed pride. He said, 'Yes,
Lucifer is guy now, a big man,' meaning that 'his' lion was
now fully adult. Symbolic as it may have been with the lions
mating, this incident brought Mohammed pleasure; a similar
pleasure to that which a father feels at his son's emergence
into manhood.

Later, after hearing the lions mate on average every
twenty minutes we all clambered on to the Land Rover's
roof to enjoy the evening.

Mohammed is the most fabulous recounter of stories and,
as the hours passed, he entertained us with tales of his years

at Kora. Amongst the many stories he told was the tragic episode of Komunyu the leopard and the Japanese film star, Tomoko, who had come to Kora with a crew to make a film about George. Strangely, she was attacked not only by one of George's lions, but also by Tony's leopard. Mohammed, an excellent mimic, using Japanese-sounding words in describing details, told how one evening the film crew were eating dinner at Tony's camp when he saw the leopard, Komunyu, enter the camp by climbing over the fence, and begin to prowl around. The leopard suddenly appeared near Tony and Tomoko and launched itself at the Japanese girl. She was seized from the back and, screaming, was pulled down as Tony attempted to pull the leopard away. At this point of the story Mohammed broke into an expressive gibberish of Japanese sounds and imitated how a huge Japanese cameraman rushed forward, tore off his shoe and, with a mighty swipe, slapped the leopard with considerable force. At this, the alarmed leopard left the girl and rushed away in fright. Tomoko, though badly injured, recovered and, with great determination, returned to finish the film.

That night, he also told for Jane's benefit, the story of Komunyu the leopard and Sam the goat. One evening, George left his camp to have supper at Tony's while a handful of camp visitors stayed at *Kampi ya Simba*. Another occupant of the camp was a young goat named Sam.

Sam's appealing nature and features had saved him from becoming food for the lions. A few hours after George left camp, Mohammed heard excited voices and, upon investigating the noise, was greeted by the sight of the visitors clambering into a parked Land Rover, shouting to Mohammed that Komunyu had climbed over the camp fence and had seized the pet goat Sam. A radio message was sent to George at Tony's camp and George rushed back to *Kampi ya Simba* to deal with the situation. Upon driving into the camp he saw the wide-eyed faces of his visitors crammed inside the Land Rover and found Mohammed attempting to persuade Komunyu to leave the goat. George then hooked the now deceased goat with a stick and dragged it as a lure for Komunyu until she was out of the camp whereupon the leopard dragged the carcass into the branches of a nearby tree. George had just closed the camp gates with a sigh when he heard the thud of a heavy object falling and turned around to see the goat lying beneath the tree just as two hyenas appeared out of the night and took off with the carcass. Whereupon George, despite the fact that the leopard had killed the camp's pet goat, was infuriated that the hyenas had made off with her kill and rushed out of the camp to pursue the hyenas. He surprised them in the darkness and, with the hyenas understandably fleeing at George's appearance, he then seized the goat and returned it to Komunyu. Such is life at Kora!

Warming to the subject, Mohammed also showed Jane and me, by torchlight, a set of deep scars on his thigh – the legacy of 'playful' games with Lucifer when the lion was eighteen months old. Mohammed explained how the lion had seized his leg as he sat on the ground.

Not wanting to excite the lion further, he had carefully placed his hands on the lion's jaws and prised them from his leg. This showed a remarkable sense of self control as by this time he had been bitten quite deeply and his legs were covered in blood. Having released the lion's jaws, he calmly, but firmly, ordered Lucifer away and limped into camp for treatment.

During the retelling of these stories, and others, the usual night sounds were punctuated by the mating snarls of Lucifer and his lioness and their sexual appetites surpassed that of hunger as neither of them ventured forward to feed upon our offering, despite the fact that a group of jackals had gathered where the goat was chained.

The following morning, leaving the carcass behind, we left the lions and returned to camp early. I told George of the situation, and Mohammed too, with joy in his eyes, spoke of his sighting of the lion. We were both determined that, if possible, George would see Lucifer for himself.

Despite the pleading of some camp visitors who wished to accompany us, I requested that only George, his tracker, Abdi, and I should return to the lions. I did not want to risk anything that might prevent George from seeing Lucifer, remembering how lions react to outsiders. We had the example of the behaviour of Growe's pride during the filming weeks.

Once we had returned to the vicinity of the lions I found that in the past two hours they had totally devoured the goat carcass. I knew that they must be lying up nearby. I drove with George and Abdi into an open area and, after much concentration and searching, I spied the lions calmly watching us from the shade of a low-spreading acacia tree.

I stopped the vehicle and pointed the lions out to George. The tracker, Abdi, instantly recognized Lucifer and became as excited as Mohammed had the night before, shaking my hand vigorously and clapping me on the back. Again I was touched by how much this lion meant to George's staff. George climbed out of the vehicle to call to them. Unfortunately, the small lioness had begun her flirtatious routine again and Lucifer, after momentarily staring, perhaps recognizing George, followed the lioness into thicker bush until both were hidden.

That morning, through perseverance, we managed to get three reasonable views of the lions, George happily confirming that it was indeed Lucifer and relieved to see that the collar had gone.

With George at last seeing the 'lost' lion, so ended the pursuit of this animal – a pursuit that had taken me many weeks, across hundreds of kilometres. My reward for the long nights of frustration was the joy in George's eyes and the satisfaction that the collar was gone.

A further reward was the knowledge that, through monitoring the lion's movements, I had discovered that

Lucifer's wanderings seemed territorially restricted to a defined area in the southern part of the reserve. During this time there had been no evidence that he had killed livestock outside the reserve, or even within it, remembering the conversation Mohammed and I had had with the young Somali herders weeks before who had, for three months, known of Lucifer and suffered no losses from him. This, to me, also dispelled any rumours that Lucifer was the young male that had reputedly leapt upon the sleeping man at Boka.

Finally, I turned the Land Rover around and headed back to camp. We were leaving Lucifer as a wild, free lion – a lion who, despite the past persecution of the Somalis and the lack of acceptance by Growe's pride, had now established himself as a territorial pride male and, in the months to come, would have progeny of his own. Thus a new pride was developing and, in turn, would grow in Kora. This is a tribute not only to the lion but also to George's and Tony's work and the result of their strong beliefs and idealism.

# 10

◄ ◆ ►

# On the Outside – Looking In

It was now early December and the rains continued steadily. Unfortunately, land utilization was being debated by government at this time, with some members of parliament stating that it was time for the government to review the structure of wildlife sanctuaries because of the growing population's demand for more land. It was put to the government that the non-viable reserves should be de-gazetted and the land given to the local inhabitants.

Because of these discussions, Kora received some bad publicity. This was published in a national newspaper article entitled 'It is Not Merely Poaching'. The article included the following statement, 'Mr Gagalo said reserves like Kora in the Tana River district were not viable and had been taken over by poachers and hippies who kept lions and flew in aircraft for unknown reasons.'

This alarmed me greatly as it had been promised that Kora would become a National Park and any negative aspects of George's project and activities could be used against him by those in government who could oppose the proposal. I knew that George would be open to criticism if the array of visitors continued to stay for long periods at camp. I felt that they brought ideals which were not relevant to the projects and were doing jobs in and around camp which belonged to the locals. Their 'residence' at Kora could all too easily produce damaging results. What, for example, would happen to George and his work if someone was attacked or injured by not heeding his warning of not venturing out of camp? And what, also, would occur if the police searched camp and found a visitor to be carrying drugs?

Unfortunately Kora, in the months I had been there, whether I could accept it or not, had acquired a reputation associated with the young visitors and one not conducive to 'active' conservation or the strengthening of the aims for the area to become a National Park. Also, with my future largely dependent upon Kora achieving National Park status, I was keen that the number and type of visitors be monitored and uninvited visitors turned away. Kora dearly needed a new image and its reputation had to be lived down if George's work and Kora's future were to build new credibility. It was desperately important that nothing threaten the chances of Kora becoming a National Park, a status which would help to ensure the protection of the area and the viable continuation of George's work which the current 'reserve' status did not afford.

I became frustrated by the situation as without a work permit I had no authority to act upon the problems. Despite this, I decided that I would risk the retribution and would try and bring some necessary change. However, my hands were tied and I wondered whether I could just let the current situation continue to the possible detriment of George and

Kora, a situation which put in jeopardy the possibility of Park status for Kora and the granting of a work permit for me.

At this time of uncertainty, we all too infrequently had visitors like Brahm at camp, but happily, during this time, Nigel Winser, expedition officer for the Royal Geographical Society, visited camp and helped break the monotony of the usual stream of people attracted to *Kampi ya Simba*.

Nigel's visit was a short-term source of encouragement for me as he had a most positive manner and we shared the same belief that Kora could have great possibilities which would, if undertaken, prove to government that Kora had a true justification for its existence.

The Royal Geographical Society once undertook an in-depth study of the ecological components of Kora and, talking with Nigel, I was keen that such important work be revived as, again, it would stress the necessity of protection for the reserve. Through such projects the area would become an 'outside laboratory' for scientists within Kenya and, internationally, this would strengthen their findings and the realization of Kora's true importance.

Back in 1983, the RGS and the National Museums of Kenya set up a camp twenty miles west of *Kampi ya Simba* on the banks of the Tana River. Twenty scientists, led by the renowned Dr Malcolm Coe of Oxford University (who subsequently wrote the book *Islands in the Bush*, which, in an entertaining way, describes the expedition) began a study which encompassed all facets, from the vegetation and the tiniest creatures to the largest mammals.

The expedition was a positive time for Kora and George as so much thought-provoking work was being accomplished and subsequent articles and reports publicized the area world-wide. The expedition also had its many comical moments.

George was often bemused by the dedicated observers,

witnessing, for example, Dr Malcolm Coe plucking a lizard from the throat of a violently protesting coucal and, when catching a python in the act of consuming a guinea fowl, leaping forward, chopping the head off the snake, and casseroling the bird!

On the serious side, over the two-year period the scientists also witnessed the effects of the relentless drought conditions and the devastation that the Somalis with their great herds were bringing to the area.

During Nigel Winser's short stay at Kora, tentative plans were made for the return of such research projects to Kora.

The rains were continuing and, despite my nagging thoughts of my future at Kora, I was delighted and felt privileged to be witnessing the resurrection of the land. It is interesting to note that two months previously, though no rain had fallen for many long months, I noticed how the acacia and commiphora trees had begun mysteriously to come into leaf. I recognized this, as I had learned in Botswana, as an omen that excellent rains were to follow soon. My predictions, mercifully, came true. Herbs and flowers of great diversity appeared overnight and their different types and colours enhanced the vibrant, alive atmosphere of the reserve.

The grass cover in Lucifer's haunts in the southern section of Kora was impressive, while those areas over-run by Somalis in the past were now being held together by a carpet of various weeds, all of which served the important role of binding the soil, and in turn gave the grass a chance to become established if good conditions were to prevail. I observed that the livestock's damage was not irreparable, especially as, under canopies of branches of thorn trees, protected from the depredations of goats and cows, grass and seed banks had become established and, with their thorny protection, were now seeding and germinating. I dearly hoped that the reserve could be continually protected from herders and their stock, then it would be possible for all the areas to recover in time. The Kora situation reminded me of a similar one I had witnessed in the North East Tuli Block in Botswana. In 1982–3 the area experienced severe drought, but was also carrying excessive amounts of grazing species such as zebra and wildebeest. It was estimated that in less than a year and a half their populations crashed by 90 per cent. Some three hundred zebra and wildebeest survived the mass starvation while two thousand seven hundred perished.

In the following seasons good rains came and the area made a dramatic recovery, high grass appearing and covering the hundreds of carcasses of those grazers which had died.

With the Somalis and their 'grazers' out of Kora, so too could this reserve recover and parts of its past dignity be restored in a phenomenon typical of such harsh lands.

With the rains, animal species within Kora were recovering condition rapidly – especially the hippos who were, at last, enjoying a deserved reprieve from conditions of old. Seeing their grass-filled droppings along the river roads made me wonder how indeed they had managed to survive at all during the previous dry conditions, when it seemed as if barely one blade of grass remained along the Tana's banks.

The rains and the change of season also brought multitudes of migrating birds to Kora – the European roller from the Mediterranean countries, the black kites from Russia and the waders like the marsh sandpipers from the Scandinavian lands, while local birds like the red-billed buffalo weavers and white-headed buffalo weavers congregated in their hundreds to breed at Kora. Male hornbills darted groundwards, seizing insects and flying, in their characteristic gliding way, to hollows in trees where the females and young awaited them.

I also found the vulturine guinea fowl were pairing off from the flocks and George told me how, for two years, these birds, because of the lack of ground cover and protection, had not bred. It was indeed a most wondrous contrast to the dry, brittle land I had entered months before.

It was amidst these sights that Jane's visit to *Kampi ya Simba* came to an end. She was to fly back to Britain happy, and excited by the possibility of returning to us on a permanent basis in due course. I, though, did not share her enthusiasm, as the possibility of Kora becoming a National Park became less definite with no announcement from the government.

Now, with Lucifer found, I rarely slept out in the bush and began to spend more time with the three cubs, working on projects such as my plans for wilderness trails and the financial adoption of the cubs, etc. At the time of Jane's visit and afterwards, I stayed at nights in a small, fenced camp a few hundred yards up the road from *Kampi ya Simba*. I lived in this camp envisaging that a large, new hut that had been built could be used as an information centre for visitors in the future.

I also accompanied Brahm on various collecting expeditions in the reserve at this time. These trips distracted me from the current worries and were also a source of interest and entertainment to George when we would return to camp, hot and tired, with tales of these adventures.

I had made a most interesting find while looking for Lucifer a few weeks previously and told Brahm about it. I had discovered upon a great flat rock shelf, pools of rain water in which fish-like creatures swam in great shoals. Brahm and I went to investigate these 'fish' further and to find where they had come from. To our astonishment, on closer examination, we discovered that they were a form of shrimp, possessed of a fascinating life cycle. On some days we would collect these creatures in great plastic bags. (I must add that I was always delegated by Brahm to venture into the ponds and risk the wrath of territorial terrapins and other inhabitants of the pools!)

Brahm would leap forward eagerly as I pulled bags filled with water and masses of red-tailed shrimps on to the rocks. He would then transfer the creatures carefully into the biscuit tins we had commandeered from George's collection in the mess hut. So it was that Brahm and I undertook a study of a most tiny facet of Kora which fascinated us both – and our findings provided much excitement.

We discovered that the shrimps were known as *stretocephalus vitreus*, and were a form of fairy shrimp. Due to the restraints placed upon them by the harsh elements, these shrimps would hatch rapidly during the rains and reach full size (nearly two centimetres) in about ten days. Their sexual development was rapid and within eighteen days egg production would take place. Obviously, the pools and the life they held shared a short tenure as the sun evaporated the water dramatically, day by day. We learnt that the eggs within the drying pools would form part of the crust with the drying algae on the levels of evaporation and would be there, in a dormant state, until the optimum conditions returned.

I had heard of a similar phenomenon in the Botswana Makgadikgadi salt pans where brine shrimps laid eggs during the rains; their eggs would also be dormant as the pans dried up and they remained resilient and unchanging despite the harsh sun and winds, and perhaps seasons without rain. But, when water returned to the pans in sufficient amounts, the cycle would begin again with the eggs hatching and the shrimps' sexual development being reached in days.

On other occasions, Brahm and I would investigate what he termed, 'the thorny problem', the world of the grossly swollen thorns of the acacia trees and their inhabitants; the larvae of moths and butterflies which lived within the tree barbs, living in a sanctuary within a sanctuary. These expeditions with Brahm would successfully push the uncertainty of my future at Kora from my mind, and for hours I would happily feel like a student on a field trip.

Around this time I also began to teach Mohammed the rudiments of driving, as a first stage towards training him as a potential trails officer. We initially lurched and stalled our way along the river roads, but very quickly, as in one possessed of an inquiring and responsive mind, Mohammed mastered the gears.

During these driving lessons I would also teach him the English names of many of the birds and trees while he, in turn, would teach me their local names, as well as the traditional medicinal uses. On one occasion he pointed out the blue commelina flowers. These flowers were used locally as natural eye drops and were complete with 'droppers'. The flat, lobular part, if pressed, and the curved end yield a few drops of clear liquid. Apparently this liquid proves effective in clearing up certain eye irritations.

It was a time of sharing knowledge, of discovering and, I hoped, a beginning of new projects to strengthen Kora's cause.

George was, at this time, totally engrossed in the cubs' progress and most of his days revolved around them. The cubs were kept within an enclosure at camp during the night and were let out into the bush early in the morning. The cubs' day began when George would open the gate on the enclosure and, as always, they would tear out excitedly towards Camp Rock, a nearby rock shelf which held small pools of water. George would, after creating some semblance of order amongst the cubs, take them, with Abdi or Mohammed, for a one and a half hour walk in the bush. The cubs would remain in the thickets below Kora Rock until mid-afternoon, when George would venture out after his ritual siesta and shower, and call the cubs in for their evening feed of goat or camel meat.

When the rains had first come, George and I watched an amusing incident with the cubs on Camp Rock. When George let them out one morning, they ran up the rock and, for the first time, discovered the pools of water. Rafiki reached the nearest pool first and lowered her head towards the water. Suddenly, she let out a spitting snarl and leapt backwards rapidly. The other two saw her reaction and trotted towards her as she approached the pool once again.

The cause of her consternation and fright, we discovered, was the horror of seeing her reflection in the water. On many occasions after this incident, all three cubs would snarl at the lion looking up from the pools before drinking.

Then, on another occasion, I remember becoming alarmed one afternoon – knowing that the cubs were resting out among the rocks – when I heard the sudden crashing sounds and cries of baboons coming from Kora Rock. One of our main fears for the cubs being out during the day was the possible threat of these apes which had previously caused havoc in the earlier rehabilitation projects.

It was suspected that baboons had killed Tony's leopard, Komunyu, trapping her upon a ledge on Kora Rock before, by sheer weight of numbers, killing her. Upon hearing the violent screams of the baboons that afternoon, I rushed out of my hut and ran through the bush towards the base of the rock, fearing the worst. I searched in vain for the cubs in the lower vegetation then spied the massing of baboons far up in the rocks.

I scampered up the cliff, rushing across the baking stone towards where the baboons had congregated. I was high up on the rocks and nearing the baboons when I heard George calling faintly from the camp far below.

I turned and looked down and, with relief mingled with amusement, saw the line of cubs walking calmly to George where he stood waving to me outside the camp. The cubs had instinctively, without any teaching, recognized the baboons as danger. They had carefully avoided them and returned, naturally, to their source of security – *Baba ya Simba* – while I rushed about gamely on the rocks trying to save them!

Feeling somewhat foolish, dripping with sweat and clasping on to the rocks and surrounded now by inquisitive baboons, I watched as George, with his usual calm, greeted the cubs in turn and led them like the saint of animals, Francis of Assisi, into their enclosure.

It was this sense of calm that I began to learn from George. George never hurried and always seemed to know the outcome of a situation, perhaps because he had lived through such occasions many times during his long years.

Christmas was drawing near and, over that period, George seemed to withdraw a little into his own world and his memories. On Christmas Day we celebrated with a turkey, marvellously prepared by Hamissi over the coals of his fire, and George, I noticed, took extra care over the wild family around him. After the Christmas lunch, I watched as he dealt out double rations of peanuts and biscuits to the hornbills, ravens, starlings, doves and squirrels and later gave the three cubs an entire goat carcass, celebrating with them in his own way the season of giving. Later he murmured to me, with wry humour, 'Well, I suppose I had better give the staff a goat as well as it's Christmas!' The staff of eight slaughtered their goat and divided it evenly while the cubs sat, initially bemused by their gift, before struggling to tear it open.

Jerry, our Irish priest friend from Kyso, came to stay at camp on Boxing Day and the evening was somewhat sad. Tony Fitzjohn's absence was very much felt by George, Doddie and Jerry.

This was one of the first Christmases he and George had not been together for some time. Jerry, with his guitar as accompaniment, sang beautiful songs of Christmas and also those of love.

Later, he began to play, more to himself than anyone, a few chords of the song, *Born Free*. George had been quiet up until that point, but suddenly, on hearing the tune, he began to sing the song, remembering the words of the music of Joy, Elsa and himself, but sadly the singing stopped as, no matter how hard he tried, Jerry could not play the entire song. The memories of the past are still fresh in George's mind, the love remains despite the years and changes. I wished that George and Jerry could have continued the song, knowing how much it meant to George and how spontaneous his singing was.

By Christmas, Growe and her pride had been away from camp for several weeks and I knew they were an important source of spiritual strength for George and he missed them a great deal. On New Year's Eve the lions showed their uncanny ability of appearing at times George most wished for them when, just minutes before we were about to celebrate the New Year, I heard, or felt, the presence of lions. I shone the torch through the camp fence and through the blackness and there, alone, was Growe. She had returned to George, their kinship acting like a catalyst, illustrating the extraordinary relationship this man shared with lions.

George was obviously delighted by her appearance and, when later we stepped together into the night to feed her, I noticed that she was particularly calm and unconcerned, despite having been away from us for so long.

She had seemingly returned to camp when George needed his spirits bolstered. As if knowing this, she had arrived. Joy Adamson had been murdered on 3 January, and it was nearing the ninth anniversary of her death. In retrospect, it is clear why I had noticed this quiet, withdrawn change in George. I had not remembered the date of Joy's death but, on the day, I could sense George's thoughts as he held private memories of their past.

All these feelings became subsidiary when we, at camp, heard the sad news that there was little hope that Kora was to become a National Park in the near future. Rumours filtered back to *Kampi ya Simba* that the Director, Dr Perez Olindo, was to leave his position. Reasons for his leaving were vague and it was thought that the National Park proposal for Kora would now be put aside for an unspecified period of time. I am essentially an optimist and, for George's sake and hopes, I tried not to believe the rumours, but was unsuccessful, as I began to be increasingly affected by the pessimism that abounded.

My future largely depended upon Kora becoming a National Park. The Elsa Trust would assist the Wildlife Department with substantial financial support if Kora was changed to the more secure National Park status, money that would be used to develop Kora and secure its future as a Park. But, without National Park status, this money would not be forthcoming, and, in reality, no position would be officially available to me.

They were indeed unsettling times, with George once again caught in the cross-fire of emotions and decisions. Because of my unofficial capacity at Kora, and because I was not able to act constructively unless Kora became a National Park, I decided that I would leave.

I could not realistically plan ahead for the proposed projects such as the wilderness trails, the self-help 'bandas', etc., if there was no money available for such projects and no hope of my now obtaining a work permit. I could not embark upon plans with George if I did not have the stability of being officially employed by him with the backing of the Elsa Trust and the government. I had arrived at Kora too late and felt that, instead of persevering, it would be best to leave Kora and George as I had found them.

Despite these feelings, George and I shared a dual concern for Kora's future, a future which he had placed upon my shoulders and which I had, then, willingly accepted.

I feel today that it was symbolic that the rest of Growe's pride duly arrived at camp at this time; first the beautiful young male, Denis, followed two days later by the six other lions. The lions remained unusually close to the vicinity of the camp until the day I left Kora.

I talked with George about my unsettled feelings and he was saddened by my predicament and worries, repeating that it was his wish that I was to be his future, Kora's future. 'Kora must not collapse when I die.' I could not help but feel deep within myself that by leaving I was deserting a quest and George. But, unless I had official capacity, there was no future for me at Kora.

I would also be leaving Mohammed and my possible contribution to his future prospects. One night, in his hut, I spoke to the man who had become my close friend about the situation. He was also adamant that I must remain at Kora or, if I had to leave, must return one day. I would be leaving the three cubs, Batian, Furaha and Rafiki, and abdicating my possible contribution to their development and welfare as they grew into their eventual wild lives.

At night, as I drove the hundred yards to my small camp where the new hut stood, complete but hollow, the pride of lions, for some strange reason, would follow me along the road, padding behind the vehicle. They would leave *Kampi ya Simba* and George and, most nights, stay for long periods resting against the camp fence, occasionally staring in from the outside to where I would sit with muddled thoughts in the candlelight of my hut.

At night the lions would stay close and I, like George, drew strength from their presence – a strength fused with sadness that I had made my final decision. I could no longer live with the uncertainty and the unsettledness and there seemed to be nothing to be achieved by prolonging my stay.

One morning, I prepared to leave. I packed my few belongings with the thought that to leave Kora suddenly, with George understanding my reasons, was better than to remain with what now seemed false dreams.

I cannot adequately describe my farewell to George, as too much welled up in my heart and, I feel, in his too. It was a torment and, with tears in both his eyes and mine, I left, thinking that perhaps it would have been kinder if we had not been kindred spirits and kinder too if I had not become anything more than 'on the outside – looking in'.

◄ ◆ ►

# Epilogue

After leaving Kenya in January 1989, I spent two months in
Britain before returning to southern Africa to write this
book. Its first draft was completed on the 31 July and I was
planning to return to George and Kora for two weeks in
October to participate in a documentary on George's life
and how we came to work together. I was so excited by this
project. It would bring us together again and would give
George the opportunity of reading this book's first draft – a
book I felt he would recognize as a tribute to him. It was a
dear wish of mine for him to enjoy its contents. The
documentary was never made, the manuscript never read.

On 20 August, a year and a day after I arrived at Kora,
George was killed while courageously attempting to protect
a camp visitor and a member of staff from a group of Somali
bandits. A violent and cruel death for a man who lived for
lions.

The news of his death numbed my being. I was devastated

by a feeling of rage, helplessness and a feeling of sorrow I have never before felt. Despite being away from George for seven months, I had, through writing this book, been close to him in spirit.

When writing about George and my experiences at Kora, the sorrow of leaving *Kampi ya Simba* was constantly relived, but it was during these months and because of the sorrow that enlightenment was born. The learning and inspiration I had drawn from George urged me to strive to embark, with renewed determination, to re-establish my own lion study project in the North East Tuli Block in Botswana. During the writing of this book, I was planning to return to where my love of lions was kindled and, from there, I planned to continue in the work of the conservation of the African lion and the wilderness itself.

While I wrote the book, I heard from friends that Kora's unstable situation was improving and that there was an air of optimism. The security forces had continued to keep the area free of Somalis and their livestock. Dr Richard Leakey had taken on the post of Director of National Parks and was attacking the extreme problem of ivory poachers with effective aggression. In March, I heard from *Kampi ya Simba* that it was planned that a permanent police camp was to be established within the reserve. George, a month before, enjoying great health, celebrated his eighty-third birthday. At this time, both Growe and One Eye gave birth to litters of three cubs each. With this, George's pride had swelled to a total of fourteen members. Batian, Furaha and Rafiki were thriving and continually brought joy to George. On hearing such news, I held some hope and optimism for Kora that it would not be long before the area was to be proclaimed a National Park.

George's death, and the nature of it, tore apart these feelings and I, amongst thousands world-wide, were stunned and shocked. George had always held life so sacred and, through the nature of his work with lions, continually promoted and protected life. He was a warm, giving man who always had to fight for his beliefs and convictions. His final action was this – a courageous attempt to protect life.

After the news of his death I was tormented by thoughts on how I could have done more to help him at Kora. This book, I had hoped, would contribute towards a more positive future for George's work and Kora. I deliberately wrote of the situation in the reserve and brought out the problem areas and how they could be resolved. It was my hope that, through highlighting the situation, I could pressure government and authorities into creating a stable situation at Kora, a situation conducive to a qualified person working with George and after him, for this was his great wish. I felt strongly that there were solutions to the problems and there was no reason why George's work must die with him.

George Adamson left a legacy to me – it is this book and, it transpired, the very essence of his work. George ended his book *Bwana Game* with the following words: 'This night I bring my story to an end. If it has the good fortune to interest anyone who may read it, they can rest assured that whatever accrues from this tale will go to aid my friends the lions.' His words apply to this tale.

As one chapter ends, the ending of a man's life intimately woven into the tapestry of an Africa of old – an Africa which is passing us by like the whisper of a desert breeze, lingering briefly and then gone – so another chapter begins. The new was conceived by tragedy, but may bring great happiness, and it begins as this tale ends.

Several days after George's death, I contacted an old friend of his in Nairobi, Monty Ruben, an Elsa Trust trustee. I, with shock and concern trembling in my voice, asked him what the future held for Kora and the three cubs. He stated that, amidst the confusion, the future was uncertain. With his reply I found myself looking inwardly. I thought to myself, 'What can be done for Kora and the cubs?' I knew that if the cubs' rehabilitation could not be continued at Kora or anywhere else in Kenya, then they would be destined to live their lives behind bars. This would be an abhorrent situation and one that George's spirit could not have rested peacefully with. His living wish for the cubs was their freedom – and this wish remained.

A day later, Monty and I spoke again. I informed him that if it was at all possible I would like to continue George's work with the cubs in the North East Tuli Block, where my future lay. I proposed to Monty to fly the cubs out of Kora and to relocate them a thousand miles to the south. There, in the Botswana bush country not unlike Kora, I would then attempt to fulfil what George would have wished for the three.

The next few weeks were a blur of meetings, discussions and of phone calls to and from Kenya, Britain, Botswana and Australia. I set out a proposal to both the Kenyan and Botswana governments and sought their approval for my plans. I sought too, sponsorship to, amongst many things, enable me to fly the cubs and myself to Botswana – both Air Botswana and Kenya Airways, each country's national carrier, quickly came forward to assist. So too did Tuli Safari Lodge in the North East Tuli Block come forward to fund all the initial costs of the project and to establish the rehabilitation camp. I had meetings with Botswana Wildlife Department officials and, with my great appreciation, I was greeted with support and approval. I made steps to set up a trust fund – the Tuli Lion Trust – as a skeleton infrastructure to build on to finance this project and other projects in the North East Tuli Block.

Finally, on 17 September, I flew to Kenya from Botswana and had planned to meet up in Nairobi with a film crew from the Australian programme, *60 Minutes*, who wished to film the cubs' relocation.

On arriving in Kenya I found myself haunted by memories of my stay there eight months before. George was no longer living, but his presence seemed almost tangible as constantly, over the first few days, I discussed my project with the authorities, government officials and friends in Nairobi.

Later, with the relocation and plans finalized, one overcast morning, I and the film crew boarded a chartered Air Kenya twin Otter and flew north-east to Kora. What was planned was that I would accompany the film crew to Kora, meet again with the cubs, talk for the film about George, the past months and the future, then fly back to Nairobi to complete the last plans in town. Then, two days later, I would return to Kora and fly with the cubs to Nairobi.

After an hour's flying time, we were low over the dry Kora landscape which was dotted occasionally with gleaming circles of elephant bones reflecting in the now clear, harsh light of the sun. As we were about to land, I thought of what we were all about to experience. The Kora situation was a volatile one. Gangs of armed *shifta* were still roaming the land. Kora's future, and my plans for the cubs, seemed balanced on a knife's edge. So easily, at any time, everything could go even further wrong in this harsh land.

As the plane landed and came to a standstill, I saw, near the two awaiting vehicles from camp and amidst a group of armed *askaris* (game department soldiers), two white men. The first, the elder, I knew by reputation. The other, I had met previously in Nairobi. The man I knew by reputation, was what I would call a 'frontiersman', one of George's oldest friends – his true friend – Major Douglas Collins. Dougie stood there shirtless, bedecked in a cloth hat, shorts and his extravagant red neckerchief. It was he who now, in his early seventies, had selflessly, upon hearing of George's death, immediately volunteered to go to Kora to look after *Kampi ya Simba* and the cubs. I call him a 'frontiersman' as I had read the book he had written, *A Tear for Somalia*. For years Dougie had lived in the wild country of Kenya and Somalia when Africa was still raw and unspoilt. The other man was Rick Matthews, a Kenyan-born young man who had courageously volunteered to assist Dougie at *Kampi ya Simba*.

As I climbed down from the plane, Rick came forward smiling and greeted us all. Introductions on the dusty airstrip were made but, to put the situation into perspective, a shotgun was given to me. 'Shoot on sight if we come across trouble on the way to camp,' Rick murmured. Dougie and Rick were living in circumstances where, at any point, those silent killers, the *shifta*, hidden in the bush, could suddenly appear and create havoc.

I moved away from the group of people and privately into my own thoughts while the loading of equipment was taking place. Dougie, sensing my low mood, came to talk to me quietly. It was as if we had known each other previously as we spoke so easily. He knew me from George's words and from the writing in George's diary. He knew too of the close bond I shared with George. Dougie told me how George so appreciated what I had tried to accomplish many months before at Kora and this meant much to me.

Dougie was from the same mould as George — a gentleman of the bush — a romantic. His character had been forged by a life of joy and heartbreak, by beauty and sadness, all intermingled with a great and desperate, infectious love of life. I liked him immediately — it was hard not to do so.

With the loading complete, we then drove in convoy to *Kampi ya Simba*. I tried to prepare myself for our arrival to a camp that symbolized the life of a man, but would now lie lifeless without that man.

As we entered the camp and I saw the staff, particularly Mohammed, waiting to greet me, I felt choked. I hugged Mohammed partially in happiness of reunion but also because of the need of strength from a friend. I hardly noticed the cameras rolling as I greeted the other staff or when I walked to the cubs' enclosure.

When I reached the fence, I was astounded by how the three lion cubs had grown in eight months. They stared at me at first with unblinking looks of puzzlement and, I felt, half recognition.

The film crew, I knew, wanted to film me meeting the cubs once again, so I stepped into their enclosure. To my astonishment the lions suddenly greeted me excitedly, moaning and groaning and rubbing their bodies exquisitely against mine. Amazingly, they had not forgotten. It made me feel that perhaps, in spirit, I had never left them or George.

Later that day, Rick drove me to George's grave and left me there a while. I did not feel that George lay under the mound of rocks next to his brother's grave. George was with me in the stir of the wind through the trees and in all the sounds around me. I felt his presence strongly and I still do. As I sat near his grave, I thought of what Mohammed had told me earlier about the grave and George's wild lions. He explained that Growe and the other lions had remained near the camp after George's death, as if seemingly they had known of what had happened. According to Mohammed, after George's funeral the wild pride had then visited the grave and some of the lions had scraped and scent-marked on the rocks. Mohammed had seen their spoor and I sensed held private thoughts on this symbolic gesture. As I sat there, my eyes began to brim with tears, but I wiped them away quickly. I couldn't allow myself to break down. So much had to be done and I had to stay strong. The time for tears would come, but only once the cubs were settled and safe. I knew, as I sat at George's grave, that tears would weaken my mind and body. Tears, at that point, would have somehow meant defeat, while from George's death I drew determination for the task ahead.

That afternoon I flew back to Nairobi and, two days later, I was back at Kora. I made preparations to load the cubs into wooden crates as we were about to start the first leg of our long journey to Botswana. Tranquillizing the cubs was traumatic but necessary. To do that task, Dieter Rottcher accompanied me. Dieter is a vet with long years of experience in animal capture. George's staff watched the darting of the cubs sullenly, unhappy at what the cubs' departure symbolized. With the cubs leaving Kora, the staff worried about their own uncertain future. The cubs' departure meant that the camp was to close until security in the area was strengthened and the *shifta* routed. As long as the cubs were at Kora, human lives were also at risk at *Kampi ya Simba*.

As Dieter and I were pulling the unconscious cubs on to blankets, I suddenly looked up and saw George's lion boy, Abdi. He was in tears. His master, like a father to him, was gone and now the children were also to go for ever. My heart went out to him. Part of me felt guilt for bringing such emotion out of the man but again I had to think positively about why the cubs were leaving. It was for their sake.

Once the cubs were loaded in the crates on the planes, the film crew and I said our farewells and left the dry land behind, leaving men with heavy hearts in a situation beyond their control. As the plane took off I saw Dougie waving, his red neckerchief still discernible in the distance. He then turned and walked back to a vehicle. Quickly though, he and the others became small, dark dots, as the immensity of the bush enveloped them and Africa became all.

At Nairobi with the cubs, I lived in a tent sited two yards from their enclosure which was part of the old Nairobi Animal Orphanage. We were together there for eleven days and, in that time, the bond between us was strengthened. Finally the day came for the cubs to leave the land of their birth and to be flown to their new home.

After arriving at Botswana's capital, Gaborone, and after a two-day rest, I, and a driver, drove the cubs, loaded in a truck, for sixteen hours. We drove through the long night and the first half of a new day. Finally, we arrived in my beloved North East Tuli Block. The cubs were 'home' and so was I.

Batian, Furaha and Rafiki have been in the reserve for over

a year now. They are almost two and a half years old and have blended beautifully into the wild life that nature dictates for them and their kind. They have learnt to be wild lions and today roam across a territory of some 150 square kilometres.

They are in a land of abundant game, permanent water and greater safety though certain dangers do exist, such as poaching – but, where is the last Eden? It is, incorporated with protection against such dangers, all they could have been given – the chance of achieving what George had wanted to give them – the chance to live free as wild lions do.

So, the last page of George's life is about to be turned, but his spirit and his legacy, three large, young lions, live on and with this the essence of his work, though sadly not at Kora, continues.

When I am out walking amongst the three lions in the wild country upon which good rains have fallen, I feel contentment. I know that what I am doing is for the right reason. As I watch the lions, their joy and well-being, I feel as though George is beside me, chuckling at his lions' boisterous games, his eyes sparkling, his spirit content. I know, as I write this, it is now as George would have wished. The freedom continues.

# Acknowledgements

Sadly, George Adamson did not read this book, nor did he hear the thanks I owe to him. He gave me so much and kindled a greater belief that man and lion can become close in spirit. His spirit lives on.

In Kenya I would like to thank all the staff at *Kampi ya Simba*. These are devoted people. My thanks go particularly to Mohammed Maru, a man of the bush who also had many of the attributes of a lion. My appreciation goes to Sue Gardner and Doddie Edmonds for their help with my project and plans. Thanks also go to Julie Marshall for her assistance during the Lucifer days. I would also like to thank Major Douglas Tatham Collins and Rick Matthews for their assistance when I returned to Kora to collect the cubs. Dougie has my great respect for what he did after George's death.

In Nairobi I wish to once again thank Joe and Simone Cheffings for their wonderful hospitality, despite the fact

167

that over the past one and a half years my arrival at their home has been often at short notice and at unusual hours. I thank Monty Ruben for all his assistance during my stay in Nairobi and Dr Perez Olindo for the time he gave me to put forward my proposal for Kora. While living with the cubs in Nairobi I was assisted kindly by Warden Sam Ngethe, Dr John Jonyo and Dr Dieter Rottcher – my thanks for all your help. Lastly, but certainly not least, I would like to express my appreciation to the Director of the Kenya Wildlife Service, Dr Richard Leakey. It was on his approval that the cubs were given to me. His position in wildlife in Kenya is one that few could fulfil and I offer him and his department my best wishes for their challenging work ahead – a work which ensures that Kenya's treasure, its wildlife, shall shine brightly as in the former years.

In Britain, my love and thanks go to my mother and stepfather, Joyce and Allan Crookshanks. Once again, great thanks are due to Jane Hunter for her love and support through the troubled times. Much appreciation goes to my agent, Tony Peake of Peake Associates and my editor, Louise Dixon of Robson Books for their assistance and work on *The Lions' Legacy*. I would like to thank Virginia McKenna for kindly providing the Foreword for this book.

In Botswana I would like to give my thanks to the Offices of the President, the Director of Wildlife and National Parks, Mr Ngwamotsoko and the Chief Wildlife Biologist, Mr Nchunga. It was they who allowed the Adamson cubs to find a home in the Botswana wilds. Special thanks go to the Gilfillan family, particularly Andrew, Hamish and William, for their support and for allowing me to continue George's work in their beautiful reserve. Great thanks are due to Tuli Safari Lodge and, particularly, to Mike Coombe-Heath, for sponsorship and support. My thanks go to all the landowners who showed enthusiasm for my work in the North East Tuli Block and to Bruce Petty and all those who greatly assisted Tuli Safari Lodge with the building of Tawana Camp (Little

Lion Camp), our home in Botswana.

In southern Africa, I wish to thank Dr Andrew McKenzie and Rozanne Savory for their encouragement and support. I thank Ruth Patterson, my stepmother, for typing the first draft of the book and my father, Roger, for giving me shelter. My thanks go to Wendy Christopher for assisting me with the text of the first draft. My love and appreciation go to Julie Thomson who picked up the pieces.

Lastly, to the lion and the passion it kindles, without which there would be no words.

# ◄ ◆ ► 
# Bibliography

Adamson, George, *Bwana Game*, Collins Harvill, 1968; *My Pride and Joy*, Collins Harvill, 1986

Adamson, Joy, *Born Free*, Collins Harvill, 1960; *Living Free*, Collins Harvill, 1961; *Forever Free*, Collins Harvill, 1962; *The Spotted Sphinx*, Collins Harvill, 1969; *Pippa's Challenge*, Collins Harvill, 1972; *A Searching Spirit*, Collins Harvill, 1978; *Queen of Shaba*, Collins Harvill, 1980 (poem on page 92 reproduced by courtesy of Harper Collins Publishers Limited

Bourke, Anthony & Rendall, John, *A Lion Called Christian*, Collins, 1971

Carr, Norman, *Return to the Wild*, Readers Union, 1963

Coe, Malcolm, *Islands in the Bush*, George Philip, 1985

Douglas-Hamilton, Iain & Oria, *Among the Elephants*, Collins, 1979

Fox, James, *White Mischief*, Jonathan Cape, 1982

Grzimek, Bernhardt, *Serengeti Shall Not Die*, Collins, 1965

Huxley, Elspeth, *The Flame Trees of Thika*, Chatto & Windus, 1959

Kaplan, Marion, *Focus Africa*, Elm Tree/Hamish Hamilton, 1983

Matthiessen, Peter, *The Tree Where Man was Born*, Collins, 1972

Owens, Mark and Delia, *Cry of the Kalahari*, Collins, 1985

Patterson, Gareth, *Cry for the Lions*, Frandsen, 1988; *Where the Lion Walked*, Viking, 1991

Patterson, R.J., *The Man-Eaters of Tsavo*, 3rd revised edition, Macmillan, 1979

Ruark, Robert, *Uhuru*, Hamish Hamilton, 1962

Schaller, George, *Golden Shadows Flying Hooves*, Collins, 1974

Thurman, Judith, *Isak Dinesen* (Karen Blixen), Penguin, 1984

# The Tuli Lion Trust

If you wish to know more about the Tuli Lion Trust – a trust dedicated to the conservation of the lion in the North East Tuli Block and throughout Africa, please write to:

> The Tuli Lion Trust
> c/o Ernst & Whinney
> P.O. Box 41015
> GABORONE
> Botswana